Exchange

Concepts in Social Thought

Series Editor: Frank Parkin

Published Titles

Concepts in Social Thought

Exchange

John Davis

University of Minnesota Press

Minneapolis

Published by the University of Minnesota Press
2037 University Avenue Southeast, Minneapolis, MN 55414

Printed in Great Britain on acid-free paper

Library of Congress Cataloging-in-Publication Data

Davis, J. (John), 1938–
    Exchange/John Davis.
        p.   cm. – (Concepts in social thought)
    Includes bibliographical references and index.
    ISBN 0–8166–2180–2 (hc). – ISBN 0–8166–2181–0 (pb)
    1. Barter. 2. Exchange. I. Title. II. Series.
HF1019.D38   1992
380.1 – dc20   92–5907
                                                              CIP

The University of Minnesota is an
equal-opportunity educator and employer.

This book is dedicated with warm friendship to
Krishan Kumar and Frank Parkin

Contents

1
Introduction

Exchange is interesting because it is the chief means by which useful things move from one person to another; because it is an important way in which people create and maintain social hierarchy; because it is a richly symbolic activity – all exchanges have got social meaning; and because for Britons and many others it is an important source of metaphors about social relations, about social order, about the fundamental processes of nature. Exchange is also often fun: it can be exhilarating as well as useful, and people get excitement from the exercise of their ingenuity in exchange at least as much because of the symbolic and social aspects as because of the material changes which may result. As you would expect, such a loaded activity is the object of social, philosophical and ethical inquiry, and people disagree about what exchange is and what its consequences are. These disputes have their own consequences, for people who try for whatever purpose to control exchange often take a view on the theoretical discussions, perhaps thinking they may be guided to success by the truths they perceive in them.

Exchange is a universal activity: it is unknown for people to produce and then consume everything directly, without any intervening exchanges at all. Many people who live in market-dominated economies have the intuition that somewhere else, among peoples without markets, producers exchange much less than we do. It is true that rural people generally eat some of their harvest, just as fishermen fry their fish and hunters chew some of their own game. In non-industrial economies, farmers may also make the string they need, and repair their mule-carts while their wives weave cloth and make pots. It is still the case that no person is self-sufficient: when a farmer produces food for a wife and eight children, he consumes one-tenth of his harvest and the rest is distributed among his family, on some terms or other. Wives always exchange with husbands, parents with children. Even if you consider a household to be the unit, which is a more complex assumption than some people think, the evidence is that households are always interdependent, and that the members exchange things with members of other households: people build houses, make tools, utensils and so on, and these often involve exchanges. And people everywhere exchange food in hospitality, in ceremony, in welfare. Some gardening households in the tropics exchanged about two-thirds of their produce, receiving about two-thirds of what they consumed, quite apart from the exchanges within their households: Trobriand households in the 1910s consumed about one-third of their product, and exchanged the rest. A high proportion of that one-third was exchanged within households. At a very rough guess, and excluding exchanges within households, most non-industrial people directly consume somewhere between two-thirds of their product, and the one-third recorded for the Trobriands. In those cases there is of course a range: children do not produce much, nor do Princes, and the incidence of exchange in their lives is greater than for other individuals. In OECD countries too the proportions vary from occupation to occupation, from town to country, from class to class: the proportion of household consumption which is produced within the household ranges from perhaps one-half to one-hundredth or less. The differences clearly exist, but it is important not to exaggerate them: at the very least the ranges overlap.

One reason we think we exchange more than some other peoples do is that we overemphasize the part which commerce plays in our lives. But it is a rather crude stereotype of our economies to think that they are overwhelmingly dominated by commerce and the state. It is rather easy to ignore all our exchanges which we make with friends and relatives rather than in a market or shop: we define them as trivial, concerned with small quantities, below the threshold of perception, even though we know from our own experience that they are politically charged, have considerable symbolic importance, and can have consequences for material as well as for emotional, spiritual well-being. Of course you recognize that 'Pass the potatoes to your mother' is a distributive act and can result in an exchange in the strict sense. It also has political and affective implications and consequences which may be quite different from 'Pass the peas to your father'. But sharing a few potatoes is surely trivial compared to buying an electric generator or selling hospital equipment? Well, yes; of course. But rather few of us buy nuclear power-stations or sell copper and coffee on the international exchanges, while most of us engage daily in formulaic domestic exchanges, buy drinks for friends, knit scarves for nephews, give and receive presents at Christmas. These exchanges are not personally trivial: observe the child who says 'I am not a servant, I'll be damned if I pass the potatoes!' And, since Britons number 55 million people or so, if we could put a money value on all of these exchanges (as some economists and accountants have tried to do) they turn out significant in vulgar cash terms as well. In most economies most people exchange most often as we do, with friends and relations. We think we are predominantly commercial, and so think that we are unlike the non-OECD world; but the differences are less than we think.

Successive governments – over several centuries – have found it easier to collect statistics in the marketplaces rather than round the dinner-tables of the nations, and our idea that we are dominated by commerce is an artefact of government's convenience: it is easier to describe market transactions, and to tax them to raise revenue, than it is to measure Sunday lunch, or children's birthday parties. The idea that the field of exchange is circumscribed by what appears in national economic statistics (the Blue Book) is a severe limitation. And to the extent that we accept it and work within that limitation we become state's men. Of course there are good practical reasons for trying to organize our households or shops or universities to accommodate effective powers; but that is no reason for allowing our minds to be limited by the state's instruments of control.

So there may be no profit in suggesting that the market is perhaps not quite such a dominant institution, or asserting that exchange encompasses more than commerce and welfare payments. But it is perhaps good for the mind if we can stretch beyond the limits of the Blue Economy, and can bring into play the accumulated evidence and analysis from those economies which are clearly not dominated by markets. The fact is that exchange is important everywhere, whether you consider the movement of useful things, whether you count the importance of exchanging as an activity in different people's lives. And it is variegated, ramified, more than we assume

when we think casually about our own economy: exchange has
political and emotional consequences which are important to
people, quite apart from the material wealth which they gain or
lose.

In 1855 the English historian Thomas Carlyle and his wife Jane were
invited to spend Christmas in Scotland at the house of a wealthy
banker, Thomas Baring, Baron Ashburton. Carlyle at that time was
famous, deeply admired, lionized in those aristocratic circles whose
stars prided themselves on their openness to culture and ideas. Lady
Harriet Ashburton – by all accounts beautiful, and certainly elegant
and condescending enough for serious writers to feel flattered by
her patronage – captured Thomas Carlyle to the extent that he
became besotted with her. Lady Harriet was concerned that her
entourage should include a renowned intellectual or two (Thack-
eray and Buller were also received at her house in Piccadilly); but
Carlyle thought that the attention he received was in some way
personal, unconnected with the prestige he conferred – in a periph-
eral sort of way – on the Ashburton household. Mrs Carlyle was not
particularly dazzled by Lady Harriet, nor indeed by Thomas: a
contemporary remarked that although no one could wish Mrs Carlyle on anyone, nor Thomas Carlyle for that matter, it was just as
well they had married each other, since otherwise they would have
made four people unhappy rather than just the two. So it was Mrs
Carlyle who pointed out the ways in which Lady Harriet maintained
social distinctions between herself and the Carlyles, even while she
showed great intellectual deference. For instance, at Christmas in
1853 or 1854 the Ashburtons' servants had refused to decorate the
Christmas tree: Lady Harriet asked the Carlyles to do it instead,
and Mrs Carlyle thought this rather high-handed. Thomas was sure
that no insult was intended, as he was when Jane pointed out that
although they travelled to Scotland in the Ashburtons' private train,
they were not admitted to the especially luxurious private carriage
where their hosts had travelled in grander style.

The Ashburtons gave Christmas presents to their guests: in 1851,
for instance, Thomas got a jigsaw puzzle, and Mrs Carlyle got a
scarf or a bracelet; that seems to have gone down quite well. But in
1855 when Mrs Carlyle unwrapped her gift, she said with considerable force that she was being insulted. She withdrew; she went to

her bedroom, and would not go down to rejoin the company until Lady Harriet had apologized, which she did 'with tears in her eyes', assuring her that she had not intended to offend. The gift which caused such upset was a black silk dress; and the reason Mrs Carlyle took offence was that at that time a black silk dress was the entirely conventional gift from an employer to an upper servant. No doubt Lady Harriet bought three or four each year, or had them made, and gave them to the cooks and housekeepers in the various Ashburton establishments, except that on this occasion she made the mistake of giving one to the notoriously prickly and sensitive Mrs Carlyle.

The first thing to notice about this story is the nature of the objects themselves. The jigsaw puzzle which Thomas Carlyle received in 1851 was then a novelty: the machinery to make them (a jigsaw which could be set to work in repetitive patterns) was a recent innovation, and the phrase 'jigsaw puzzle' did not become common usage until the 1870s. Similarly with mass-produced clothing (if that is what Mrs Carlyle's was): ready-made, off-the-peg black silk dresses were a novelty. However, the puzzle was a quite new kind of object, one which did not exist until the technology had been invented; while clothing was produced by machines which replaced a direct and personal human service: it was a bit like buying tinned baked beans, or any processed food. So, if Lady Harriet had bought the dress in a shop, two quite different consequences of manufacturing innovation are involved, and these are likely to result in rather different social evaluations. For it seems (I have no evidence for this at all) that however impersonal jigsaws were, they were from the beginning a social toy: solving the puzzle was perhaps never a solitary pleasure. A black silk dress does not afford such prospects of intimacy: it is personal, and cannot be shared. And to give a manufactured dress (or even one made by a dressmaker) rather than a bespoke one, suggests that in the eyes of the giver it didn't really matter much whether it was a good fit or not: Lady Harriets, it implied, couldn't conceive that Mrs Carlyles thought about elegance and comfort. So, the nature of the gifts suggested some differentiation between husband and wife; and although Mrs Carlyle was by no means one heart and mind with her husband, it is hurtful when someone else perceives it and acts upon it, and makes no bones about it.

In addition, there seems to have been an element of class

distinction. Lady Harriet was exceedingly wealthy; the Carlyles were upwardly mobile middle-class people whom the Ashburtons would not know – except that Thomas Carlyle was a giant of the intellect, and hence acceptable in a salon. Nobility could confer temporary and strictly circumscribed equality on such persons, the aristocracy of wealth empowered to elevate the lords of intellect, provided that they were prepared to do semi-menial jobs (like decorating a Christmas tree) when asked. Lady Harriet was prepared to elevate the Intellect, but not its wife. Mrs Carlyle however thought that she was entitled through matrimony to the same rank and privileges as her husband; and although she resented her husband's besottedness with the woman he called his 'goddess', and said that he was blinded to her insults by it, perhaps she was not simply jealous. It is at any rate possible that she and Lady Harriet had different views of marriage: one of them thought that marriage entailed equality of treatment, and the other hadn't considered the possibility of any such thing.

A jigsaw puzzle and a dress are a fairly simple and apparently straightforward pair of gifts. In order to explore why one was proper and the other deeply wounding, you have to look at the meanings which the people attributed to objects; and to uncover those, you have to consider manufacturing innovation, and how it gave rise to new products in the one case, to displacement of direct personal service in the other. And then you have to consider a class structure which had aristocrats with upper servants to whom they gave not quite sufficiently caring tokens of esteem: gifts which kept them in their place. And it included too the upwardly mobile, the middle-class intellectual, acceptable because he was defined as Genius. But mobility caused discrepancies and misunderstandings, confusions about who defined the terms and who was included and excluded; and these issues in turn seem to hint at different notions of matrimony and marital solidarity – which in this case were particularly sensitive because of the strained relations within the triangle. A simple gift has meanings which involve class, social mobility, matrimony, patronage, employment, manufacturing processes, issues of style, and of changing rituals or conventions of gift-giving. This encapsulation is a general characteristic of all exchange everywhere: it is not confined to nineteenth-century Britain, for you can trace out similar kinds of connections in all societies.

This is a controversial point, for many economists and economic anthropologists suggest that in industrial market economies exchanges are somehow less embedded than they are in pre-industrial non-market ones. Marcel Mauss started this line of thought in his book *The Gift*, when he argued that potlatch – a series of exchanges described in particular by Franz Boas after his field trips to the Indian groups living near Vancouver – was a *prestation totale*, an exchange which involved the total social personalities of the exchangers. The suggestion is that our market exchanges are more impersonal, less is at stake, the ramifications are less than *totale*. And potlatch or *kula* are in fact really very different from a shopping expedition to your local supermarket. However, it seems that it is a matter of more encapsulation and less, rather than either and or. Anyway, the first point to make about embeddedness is that to one degree or another, it is a universal characteristic of exchanges.

The symbolic, moral, legal, ritual meanings of exchanges, and their ramified institutional connections are usually fairly clearly patterned. They are not arbitrary, casual, random. This too is a controversial point to make, for the general non-anthropological view of exchange is that it is always in essence rational and profit-motivated: it is essentially market-like, and that is what is important about exchange. In this view the embeddedness of exchange is a distortion of its underlying market-likeness. In the language of neo-classical economics, those institutions such as Christmas, kula, the potlatch, are manifestations of imperfection, things which can be ignored or discounted when you make a formal model of economic actions and their consequences. 'Other things being equal', the marketist says, the economy will perform as the model predicts. The facts seem to be first, that economies rarely perform as the model predicts; 'other things' never are equal. And then secondly, it also seems fairly clear that those other things – the institutions, moral evaluations of goods and relationships, symbolic orders – are not random or arbitrary, but are patterned, coherent within reasonable limits of tolerance, and are consequential.

So in the next chapters I attempt an account of exchange which emphasizes the moral and symbolic order, the meanings with which people invest their actions; the slogan is 'other things are never equal, and are always patterned'. Consequentiality is located not in the working of economic laws, but in the social rules of power, symbol, convention, etiquette, ritual, role and status. This is also a little bit subversive of current trends in anthropological analysis. For many anthropologists have adopted one or other of two main paths which lead round the issue of market rationality. One, which you might call *du côté de chez Sahlins*, is a noble and innovative argument deriving from Polanyi and leading through Dalton to Sahlins and Godelier. It says, roughly, that market models are adequate for Western industrial economies, but other economies need different models because they are based on other principles. I argue that OECD economies are also based on other principles. The second path, *du côté de chez Strathern*, concentrates on symbols and meanings: all else is unreal – only social constructions, the meanings construed on objects and actions, are truly real. This too is an ancient line drawn from Herder through Wittgenstein: it results in fine analyses of different mental worlds (although you may sometimes think that the language we use to analyse symbols is insufficiently sharp to allow precision). But in any case I want to ask why it is that out of all this mental activity some of us get wooden jigsaws to play with, others silk dresses to clothe our nakedness in, while others still lack food and a roof, and a special train with a special saloon carriage. Mentalist principles have not been used to explain vulgar differences, I think; and as yet we do not know why some symbolic worlds produce cooked breakfasts, and others do not.

Kinds of Exchange

In June 1918 in the Trobriand Islands two men quarrelled about their harvests: one, from Kakwaku village, disparaged the other's yams, suggesting he was a bad gardener; the other, from Wakayse, returned the insult. Their chiefs intervened to make peace, but unfortunately they too lost their tempers: Kakwaku said in effect that Wakayse really did not have decent gardens. So, to prove them wrong, the chief of Wakayse got his people to erect a crate ('4.6 metres long, 1.85 metres wide and 1.7 metres high') in Kakwaku, and then they filled it with yams, putting some specially decorated giant prize specimens on top. That was their challenge – 14.5 cubic metres of yams, excluding the monsters. The next day Kakwaku villagers brought the crate back to Wakayse, and filled it with about the same quantity of their yams: they said they had seriously considered exceeding the original amount, but had held back because that would have been too insulting. Some sort of peace prevailed.

Trobrianders called this exchange of yams *buritila'ulo*. They did not do it very often; they had many ways of transferring yams from one person to another, and buritila'ulo was the channel for a minute proportion of the flow of yams: it was relatively insignificant among the eighty or so named kinds of exchange which Trobrianders recognized. It was an exchange between villages: each member of the insulted village contributed his harvest, and expected his share of the yams of the village which had made the insult. It was also an exchange of a particular kind of thing – mainly yams and monster yams, but with some small amounts of sugar-cane and betel added. And finally, it contained a rule of exchange: the conventionally polite return from the insulters was an equal amount of similar objects. To underdo was a humiliation since it showed the original insult to have been baseless and vainglorious; while to overdo the return was 'a declaration of war' since it asserted that the insult had been justified. Malinowski recorded that serious fighting had broken out in the past, between villages not such close neighbours as Wakayse and Kakwaku. Buritila'ulo was thus distinct from other kinds of exchange: while villages exchanged with each other on other occasions, and while Trobrianders often exchanged yams, and while exact equivalence was polite behaviour in other exchanges, only buritila'ulo had the particular combination of village plus yams plus equivalence. On other occasions Trobrianders did give good measure as a sign of goodwill, trust, friendliness, and in the expectation of getting good measure in return. But in buritila'ulo, good measure was threatening.

You may agree that those Trobrianders thought and acted within a world in which buritila'ulo was an infrequent but distinct exchange: no doubt a nuisance brought about by the hot tempers of people who, if only they had been cooler, could have spared everyone the trouble. But once it had begun, involving the prestige, the efforts and all the yams of the two sets of villagers, it seemed to them distinctive, an instance of buritila'ulo rather than one of *gimwali* or kula or any of the other named kinds of exchange which Trobrianders had in their repertoire.

The problem with that is that many economists and some anthropologists do not accept that there can be kinds of exchange. Marketists argue that only one real kind of exchange exists, which is profit-motivated exchange. Other forms are only apparent since they are the product of institutional quirks, of social distortions which introduce imperfections. And some anthropologists argue that although kinds of exchange exist, in any particular social group only one is dominant. For instance, the justly renowned Professor Sahlins argues that just as capitalist countries are dominated by markets and the profit motive, so Trobrianders had a 'reciprocal' economy – one dominated by the principle of 'giving good measure'.

What these two kinds of argument have in common is, they deny the conceptual autonomy of (in this case) buritila'ulo and say that it is really something else. In all other respects the two arguments are incompatible, and the proponents of the one and the other are antagonistic. But they share the notion that Trobianders' or any other natives' statements are in some cases untrue. (They are less knowing when a native says something which fits their models.) So, on the one hand, Trobrianders' elemental rationality was distorted and made imperfect by their relatively unspecialized economy: they could not pursue profit directly, but had to do so through institutions such as buritila'ulo which effectively concealed the workings of the profit motive – from Trobrianders as well as from anthropologists. Similarly, if the natives of England say they engage in reciprocal exchanges, they must be wrong: once again, social convention requires that their profit-seeking is masked from the participants in, say, a Christmas party. I argue that the perceptions of British or Trobriand natives are substantially correct: we have available to us a range of different kinds of exchange – a repertoire of socially acceptable practices which are culturally, morally and even economically distinct.

One of the more elaborate and complex exchanges available to some Trobrianders is kula: a kind of exchange which links Trobrianders among themselves, and also creates inter-island alliances. It was described in great detail by Malinowski as well as by many others, and was established by him as an archetypal reciprocal exchange.

Kula objects were (still are) armshells and necklaces which conventionally had to be exchanged against each other. Important Trobrianders exchanged kula objects with their dependants in the Trobriands, and with those whom they wished to put in that position. With these men they also exchanged in other ways. And they had exchange partners on other islands with whom kula was their main kind of exchange: they visited their partners from time to time, and received them at home. Visitors expected a gift of a kula valuable.

All the participants in kula exchanges seem to have considered some kula things more valuable than others, and to have agreed more or less which these were; and the rule was that a man who received a necklace on an overseas visit should reciprocate with an armshell of equal or greater value when his partner returned the visit. So Trobrianders' partners in a south-west-ish direction gave them necklaces, which the Trobrianders took home and then gave away again a few months later when they received visitors from the Marshall Bennett Islands, from the north-east. When Trobrianders visited their partners on Marshall Bennett they received armshells, took them home, and gave them away when they received visitors from the south-west.

Malinowski, the first to describe kula in any detail, emphasized the circularity of the exchanges: some fourteen groups of islands were involved in kula, and they formed a ring: necklaces travelled roughly clockwise, armshells anti-clockwise, each object completing a circle in from two to ten years, depending mostly on the numbers of intra-island exchanges it was involved in.

Partners who could not match the value of a kula object which they had received, offered a holding gift – a token of good intent – but could be expected to meet the obligation because they would pass the valuable object on, and eventually receive something valuable in return. Indeed, they used this technique to create indebtedness: if a Trobriander heard that a partner in the Marshall Bennett group had, or expected to have, a specially fine armshell, he could hint as much to a partner on (say) Dobu, in the hope of getting a fine necklace from him. If he was successful, he could use the necklace to extract the armshell from the Marshall Bennetter. For each important islander had several overseas partners, and had to choose to which of them he would give the more or less valuable objects in his temporary possession. Kula objects therefore passed through different hands on each circuit, and the important men in each group of islands competed with each other, trying to ensure that the more valuable objects came to them and not to their rivals. The prestige got by success in that competition was an important asset in a relatively fluid political society; and the objects themselves could be exchanged with dependants in the Trobriands, used to build a local following.

In the seventy or so years since Malinowski's research anthropologists have increasingly emphasized the actors' points of view: instead of thinking of kula primarily as a ring on which kula goods circulate, we pay attention to the schemes, coups, wheezes, fantasies with which men on the islands plot their future success and renown. Indeed, E. R. Leach (in a characteristically dialectical essay) suggested that

> There is no such thing as THE KULA. It is rather that in the geographical zone which has come to be regarded as the kula area there is a certain general similarity about the ways in which non-utilitarian 'valuables' . . . are 'traded around'.

The point is that at least some goods do travel round the ring; and islanders are pleased when a known object reappears as it should.

But modern analysis suggests that they are not primarily servants of the ring, but manipulators of paths, or *keda*s. A keda is the path on which a kula valuable travels, from one man to another to another. The markers of a path are usually previous exchanges: a man gives because he has received, and gives because he wishes to oblige some other person to give him what he wants. So the keda is the list of flesh-and-blood people who transmit valuables; it is also a list of obligation – A has been obliged to B, who has been obliged to C. . . . And thirdly, it is a set of expectations about the future: A sends a valuable along the path because he wants something from E or F or G; and he knows that C is obliged to B, and will be more so when B gives him A's valuable, and that D is similarly obliged to C, and so on.

The risk and the possibilities of manipulation arose from two sources. First, some kula valuables were free from existing obligation: as Malinowski described kula, all valuables were permanently pre-empted by existing obligations. Anthropologists do not know whether he overlooked the significant category of untied valuables (*kitoum*) or whether it was a later creation by Trobrianders and others. But in the 1970s, at least, it existed and it provided kula operators with an important source of freedom: with a kitoum they could create new paths or they could resurrect old ones. And they could falsely represent a tied valuable as an untied one.

The second source of risk and manipulation was that most participants in kula exchanges were involved in more than one path: as initiators or as intermediaries, they had several kedas going at once, and were like knots in a complex net. A participant in one keda could divert valuables to another if he thought he would gain by doing so, for instance if he thought the partners in the original path were less important than those in the diversion; or if he needed to use a really good valuable to satisfy pressing demands elsewhere. Rerouting, passing a tied valuable as untied, were tactics he could use for satisfying some associates at the expense of others. The risk was that his associates would do it to him, demonstrating that they considered their obligations to him less important than their obligation to some others.

Participants in kula were shamed if they held on to valuables – they had to use them in exchange; and they had to try to ensure that their paths did in fact produce the equal return they were after. A successful series of transactions was one in which a man sent out a kitoum which eventually brought back a particular intended equivalent valuable; and the success indicated that his partner, and his partner's partner, and his partner's partner's partner (and so on) were all trustworthy people who held each other in respect and who did not manipulate the valuables: even at three or four or five removes a man's intention had held, because the partners wanted to play his path rather than anyone else's. A successful series of kula transactions was therefore a quite remarkable testimonial. And to start one off (which was difficult to avoid) was highly risky: people lived on tenterhooks, among other reasons because they knew that everyone else in their home group was watching and commenting, some of them rivals for esteem who would be quite happy if everything went wrong.

The subtlety of kula exchange is clear; so too are the diplomatic and economic skills which a partner needed if he was to be successful. Trobrianders regarded kula as a distinct kind of exchange, surrounded it with unique ceremonial and etiquette. The exchangers were partners, and at any rate on overseas expeditions did not exchange much else than valuables. The objects were strictly prescribed, and were almost solely used for kula exchanges. The rule of exchange was that partners should match values, or exceed them on the principle of giving good measure. That was different from buritila'ulo, in which the exchangers were antagonistic villages (not individuals linked in partnership), in which they exchanged multi-purpose yams (not valuables with limited exchangeability), and 'good measure' was threatening.

So buritila'ulo and kula were distinct types of exchange in Trobriand eyes, and (together with others) they made up a repertoire of exchanges. I argue that Trobrianders' understandings of what they did is a central datum, and that arguments to the effect that they deceived themselves and were really doing something else are generally shoddy.

It is now necessary to remark that anthropologists and economists have not often directly confronted each other by producing alternative analyses of the same material. On the one hand anthropologists have often taken neo-classical economics for granted, and have worked by leaving OECD economies to economists: they have been content to leave them their sphere of action and to point out that other economies do not fit their analyses. On the other hand, economists have not bothered to come to grips with the evidence from non-OECD countries, beyond occasional references to Mauss and Malinowski which do not reveal careful reading. In consequence, it is not possible here to confront two analyses of the same data. The second-best procedure is to examine the work of some marketists who have discussed analogous issues: the case of charity and altruism suggests itself, and in particular the discussion of blood donors serves to illustrate their characteristic approach to exchanges which ostensibly are integrated by something other than market rationality.

The arguments about blood donors were stimulated by a direct and important policy issue in Britain in the 1960s: how to get more blood for the National Health Service. Some people thought the best way was to stimulate people's free and altruistic donations; others thought the best way would be to pay them (as blood banks do in the USA). To support this policy they attacked the ideas that donors are free and altruistic. They argued that altruists are not free because they are constrained to give their blood by social pressures from friends, colleagues at work, and advertising. That is true; but it is an argument of much wider application, for it applies to most social activities, including market choices which are therefore not free either. So you cannot say that altruists are bound and marketers are free, because the criterion applies equally to each of them and does not discriminate between different sorts of economic activity. The marketists also argued that donors were not altruistic because they did in fact make a profit. Blood donors had some minor costs – time, a transitory pain perhaps, and the possibly unwelcome sight of tubes and bottles. But in return they got a cup of tea, contact with friendly and grateful medical personnel, and an inner reassurance that they had done a good deed, had contributed to the well-being of some unknown unfortunate. Those were rewards, incomings; and if you could account for them, you would see that the people who donated blood were making a profit: their costs were less than their rewards. So: to pay money to blood donors would not be a radically commercial innovation because a donor's altruism was only apparent. Nobody denied that the rewards were fairly small; and that they would be insufficient for people who had less time to spare, or were more squeamish than the existing pool of donors. To attract those people the transfusion service should therefore increase the rewards: for instance, they could pay cash.

The discussion was ramified. What is important for present

purposes is that here is an argument that kinds of exchange do not really exist: native Britons might distinguish between selling blood and giving it, but social scientists could see that there is no real distinction between these exchanges, and that donors were really profit-motivated.

The issue is partly whether blood donors are motivated by altruism or by profit. It is always difficult to know what another person's motives may be: it is perfectly possible that some healthy people value very highly a fleeting contact with a doctor or nurse and that they give blood for that reason rather than to aid an injured person. But that is scarcely an argument against the existence of altruism in Britain. Suppose someone told lies about his reasons for being a shopkeeper, or about his balance sheet: would that be evidence that commerce does not exist? What anthropologists do in such circumstances is to ask other people: Ahmad sends money off to relieve distress, and you tell the neighbours 'Ahmad has sent 10 dinars to Cyprus'. 'Did he say so? Did he show you the receipt? That's not true alms' (*zakat*). 'True alms' is a category, and Ahmad's neighbours discussed with alacrity and some malice whether or not his gift to Cyprus came into it: the discussion established the notion of 'true alms' as a reality. Ahmad's fellow tribesmen in Libya showed the same scepticism about his claims to have made fantastic profits on his trading journeys. But no one doubted that both 'alms' and 'trade' exist, and that you can tell what is which. So the argument that some people may have the wrong motives for exchanging in a particular way, or that they tell lies about their motives or the outcome, is not an attack on the notion that there are kinds of exchange. The (probable) fact that Ahmad told lies about his commercial success does not cast doubt on the existence of trade as a kind of exchange.

What about the immaterial reward – that inner sense of well-being and the external reputation that comes from acting rightly? That surely is real – can it go in the accounts on the credit side? Tullock has remarked that 'A decision to make a charitable donation is no more economically irrational than a decision to buy a car. Both are ways of using income to "purchase" satisfaction; both increase utility (of the purchaser)'.

In the first instance, that is a way of looking at charity (rewarded by God) and altruism. The metaphor does not correspond to what at least some people think about their actions. For instance, one contributor to the relief fund for the disaster which struck the Welsh village of Aberfan in 1966 wrote: 'Please use this small amount in any way you wish. I was saving it up for a new coat, O God I wish I had save more'. It is extraordinarily unlikely that this anonymous person thought she was 'purchasing' satisfaction for herself: she experienced a movement of the spirit; suffered anguish at the sorrow of others; sacrificed her coat and continued to wish she had more to contribute. That is at least some part of the reality. It is also quite possible that her anguish diminished as she felt she had done something to help, but it is difficult to argue that she sent her savings because she recognized that as the price to pay for the relief of some part of her anguish. However, suppose she did have that intention: you might then say 'that was not true charity because she was more concerned with her own relief than with disaster relief'; you would not say 'that disproves the existence of charity (or altruism)'. The category exists, and we can all imagine cases which would fall into it.

Of course people can talk about altruistic actions in any way they choose – as if they all are commercial, or are all governed by some hidden genetic compulsion, or are all causes of the distress they seek to relieve. It is amusing; it can shock people who are self-assured of their own righteousness. But these are never more than ways of talking, and it is very difficult to sustain an argument to the effect that such metaphors are more real than the intentions and purposes of people who explain and justify their actions. 'The purchase of satisfaction' is a metaphor, and is not really what people do.

The claim that it is real, or more real, is a conjuring trick which depends on three simultaneous sleights of mind. The first is what may be called Salimbene's Paradox.[1] It is an abstraction of a quite common kind of introspection which still seems to be common among some educated and scrupulous persons: 'I have been truly altruistic (I am not as other men are). If I can even think that, then I am not truly altruistic. But if I can criticize myself for thinking that, it is reassuring (I am not as other men are). If I can even think that, then I am not truly altruistic . . .'. Some economists argue that

---

[1] Salimbene of Parma was a witty and sardonic Franciscan chronicler who flourished about 1250. I attribute to him, though I am not sure I am right to do so, the comment that the election of a contemporary pope must have been by the direct intervention of God because there was no earthly reason the cardinals should have chosen him. Whoever made the joke, I take it as emblematic of the position that only *actes gratuites* are candidate members of the category 'unquestionably good actions'.

Table 1   Notional accounts of an altruist and a shopkeeper
(version 1)

	Dr	Cr
Altruist		
Donation	£1.00	
Return		Ex
Profit		Ex−£1
Shopkeeper		
Purchase of stock	£1.00	
Overheads	£0.40	
Sales		£1.60
Profit		£0.20

Units are pounds sterling (£) and economical esteems (E). The
exchange rate is not known.

people are pleased with themselves for being altruistic, and so they
are not altruistic: they elevate that dreadful antiphony of regressive
self-examination, which is a hallmark of adolescent uncertainty and
self-doubt, to the status of an axiomatic foundation for the analysis
of economy. Most people grow out of it, because the inevitable
conclusion of such an analysis, whether by adolescents or by
economists, is that the only good actions are those which have no
purpose or aim at all, and hence can have no conceivable measure of
success or failure, and hence cannot cause satisfaction in the person
who does them. That is clearly an absurdity.

The second trick is contained in the accounting procedures used
to support the notion that altruists and alms-givers are profit-
making purchasers of satisfaction. Imagine the accounts of an
altruist and a shopkeeper. They presumably look something like
Table 1. If altruists are profit-motivated their incoming esteems
must be greater than their outgoing pounds or dollars. But although
marketists do assume that altruists' accounts show a profit, no one
has tried to evaluate esteem (self-satisfaction, reputation); and it
should make any auditor suspicious that in these accounts esteem is
an item whose value varies always sufficiently to show a profit.
Marketists are not necessarily wrong to include esteem in the

Table 2   Notional accounts of a shopkeeper (version 2)

	Dr	Cr
Purchase of stock	£1.00	
Overheads	£0.40	
Sales		£1.60
Esteem		E*x*
Profit	£0.20 + E*x*	

accounts, but they should take care to show that they are not cooking the books; and they do not.

A further problem with the accounting procedure is that in fact shopkeepers and industrialists and farmers and traders also get considerable satisfaction when they do a good deal; and they may also get reputation – some are ennobled, for instance. So they too should have esteem in their accounts (Table 2). The true and fair accounts should have an *x* in both series, since both commerce and altruism create esteem. So economists who include only the altruist's esteem are cooking the books twice over. If they tried to reflect the real state of affairs, they would have to show two unknown quantities: the atruist's *x* always great enough to show a profit; the shopkeeper's *x* always small enough to ensure that his total of cash and esteem does not outweigh the altruist's net gain. If marketists put their *x*s into both baskets, as they should, their calculations would be even more risky.

So the suggestion that 'esteem' is an income which can contribute to the profits of an enterprise suffers from another defect. For reputation in the eyes of others distinguishes success from failure – good shopkeepers from bad ones, good altruists from those whose works spread terror and dismay rather than comfort and joy. It does not distinguish gratuitous actions (*alla* Salimbene) from purposeful or interested ones. There is no reason to withhold esteem from an altruist, simply because he is good at altruism. I admit that self-regard is a more difficult matter, since people do exist whose complacency seems independent of any external reference. Even so, the best thing to do, while the world still lacks accurate measures of self-regard and reputation, is to hold them constant between kinds of exchange: perhaps people, or some people, do esteem kula-ists more highly than they do buritila'ulo-ists, and blood donors more highly than shopkeepers. But until measures exist, it seems unwise to base such fundamental arguments, that altruists' immaterial rewards always outweigh their costs, on intuitive assessments which could be prejudiced.

The third sleight is a three-way pun on 'rationality', which has different senses, allowing users to slip from one to another without notice. I may have rational purposes (to do or make something); and I may pursue those aims in a sensible or a silly way; and I may, in economic usage, be rational by aiming to increase my utility (I may be profit-motivated). The pun allows sophists to show that all purposeful action is profit-motivated. In some cases it is clear that the three senses coincide: a shopkeeper can be rational in all three senses without offending any of our usual understandings of 'rational'. But Britons, and probably most other Westerners, would usually say that an altruist can be rational in only two of the three senses: he sets a sensible goal; he goes about achieving it in a sensible way; and he makes a loss. You have already seen how that loss can be converted to a profit by applying Salimbene's Paradox, and by cooking the books with the magical ingredient Esteem. The third way is by assuming that what is rational in the first two senses is generically rational, and hence profit-motivated. That insinuates a false equivalence because profit motivation is here axiomatic and the other two senses are not. So, you can argue about the rationality of aims ('He wants to go to the moon tonight') and about the rationality of means ('So he is practising the long jump') because you know what would be irrational. But rationality-profit has no corresponding irrationality: it cannot be, for instance, irrationality-loss, because you know (by the terms of the argument) that a person who truly wants to make a loss is profit-motivated; and one who wants to make a profit but who in fact makes a loss has only made a mistake.

This combination of Salimbene's Paradox, false accounting and multiple punning is the basis of very elegant argument and moderately elevated mathematics; but it is no more than a metaphor, a way of talking about exchange as if it were always profit-motivated. It has some value because it is very provoking, and forces us to think about our actions and motives. Moreover, you could say that, if a social science is to be a servant of government and policy, it is better to have one guaranteed to be merely metaphorical, rather than a science which makes states more efficacious. But neo-classical economics is a science fiction: nineteenth-century economists tried to imagine how the world would be in the worst possible case they could imagine, and demonstrated to their own satisfaction that life would still be tolerable if everybody was concerned only with their private gains. Unfortunately many economists and state's men have come to believe that ancestral nightmare is a true description of our intentions and actions; and they try to mould the world accordingly. Edgeworth's Bad Dream becomes a goal.

This is not the place to inquire into the mental process which allows economists and politicians to transmute a nightmare into an idyll. But it is useful to point out that effective models are not all as good as each other. It is a popular and in many cases convincing argument that a model is just an intellectual construct: provided it accounts for a reasonable selection of facts in a moderately satisfactory way, you do not have reasons to prefer another. That is an attractive argument to any person, intellectual or other, who likes making patterns, as most of us do: anyone is entitled to describe the world *as if* it were flat, or made by a god, or made out of blue cheese. Every person is entitled to play with his patterns. But this is not all that marketists do. First, humans have a common propensity to elevate their models when they are reasonably pleasing: we come to believe that what was originally a metaphor is real, true and has an existence outside our minds. This propensity to derive the *as is* from the *as if* is common to humanity as a whole: to observe that marketists suffer from it reminds us that they are within the pale. But the consequences of this particular model, when it passes for real, are quite serious. It would have no consequences for public policy particularly, if state's men thought that the world was really made of cheese. But they are concerned to control exchange and to tax it, in order to finance their dedication to the common good. A simple description of reality, which puts one or two handles within their grasp, has consequences which are less debated than they might be. When state's men can appeal to natural laws to justify their actions, they cause an intellectual impoverishment, since the world comes to seem flatter than it is. That is quite apart from any consequences their beliefs may have for the livelihoods and spiritual well-being of the people they try to control.

To return to the main theme. When economists say that altruism or charity 'is not to be separated easily into a category in a higher moral plane than selling' (Institute of Economic Affairs, 1973, p. vi), they think they have successfully levelled 'O God I wish I had save more' down to show how similar it is to the corner store. You buy pâté in Harrods, and you get your self-esteem at your local charity shop. But I have argued that both commerce and altruism attract moral judgement, and are not separated easily on that accounting: shopkeepers earn reputation just as philanthropists do, by being successful in their transactions. Up to a point: people should conduct themselves successfully in a range of types of exchange; and the shopkeepers who are ennobled are generally those who are also notably successful philanthropists.

Note the consequences of this argument for the Trobrianders and their kula. The blood-donor discussion, transposed to the Pacific, casts Trobrianders as profit-conscious entrepreneurs thwarted by cumbersome primitive institutions, and constrained by imperfection-creating etiquettes to engage in irrational rigmaroles. The esteem which a kula-ist got from his exchanges was a 'profit': it was an important political resource which he could use elsewhere in Trobriand life – in politics, in marriage arrangements, and hence in the accumulation of wealth. Instead of pursuing economic profit directly, Trobrianders had to pursue political and social prestige first; and when they had that, they were better able to create and maintain wealth. That of course further inhibited perfect competition, since it created restricted access to goods and services and excluded the majority of the population from free access to the market in yams or pots or women or betel nuts.

That is one way of talking about Trobriand kula exchanges: it is based on a series of conjuring tricks and on an assumption that what Trobrianders say about their actions is untrue or misleading. They say that kula is based on giving an equal or better return, and is quite different from buritila'ulo or any other kind of Trobriand exchange. I have argued that of course Trobrianders like to be esteemed; and they are delighted when a keda strategy works as they intended it should; but this is not 'another kind of profit' which substitutes for cash in the bank because people with cash in the bank also have esteem.

It is time to consider another wrong and important analysis of Trobriand exchange. This has been elaborated most clearly by

Professor Sahlins. He builds on long and powerful traditions which reject what used to be called formal economic analysis (but you have just seen how informal it really is), and to some limited extent accept the value of what natives say. Sahlins agrees that Trobrianders tried to achieve equality or 'good measure' in their kula exchanges, and in various others as well: mothers who suckled their children, were giving 'pure gifts' in abundant good measure, as were Trobriand fathers who passed on knowledge and goods to their children (to whom, in the Trobriand kinship system, they had no material obligation; and from whom they had no expectation of return).

Sahlins's argument, made from a genuine and inspiring 'dialogue with ethnographic materials', is that some economies are based on reciprocity, just as some are based on market exchange. Reciprocity is not a single relation between incomings and outgoings, but a 'continuum', a 'spectrum', ranging from the pure gift of suckling, in which 'the expectation of a direct material return is unseemly', to barter and theft which are each an 'attempt to get something for nothing with impunity'. In between are those balanced reciprocities in which social conventions 'stipulate returns of commensurate worth or utility within a finite and a narrow period'. Kula comes into this middle category.

Trobrianders (like many others) did give freely to those who were closest to them in kinship terms; they were more calculating givers to those who were more distant but still within the horizon of social order; and they were unscrupulously self-interested and oriented to short-term returns when they dealt with people who were beyond the bounds of kinship and control. But, according to Sahlins, all these are forms of reciprocity when they occur in a reciprocity-dominated economy. Similarly, persons with political authority organized exchanges within their own social group: such exchanges were structured by authority, and constituted 'pooling'. This was a form of taxation and welfare distribution; and it was reciprocal because, for instance, political authority in those societies which have reciprocity-based economies is founded in kinship. Chiefs derive their claims to authority from a position of seniority among kinsmen, or cast them in a kinship idiom of parental privilege and responsibility: Sahlins argues that exchange organized by kinship entails 'giving good measure', and is therefore reciprocal.

In Sahlins's hands this account of reciprocity is the basis for a brilliant and unique attempt to create an economics of reciprocity – to work out the principles of 'price' formation and fluctuations in trade in a reciprocal economy. It is a *tour de force* which excites admiration in most of his readers. In some, however, it is a contestatory admiration; and so it should be in all of them. For the defects of this argument are two. First, it denies the possibility of a unified and accurate account of exchange: it requires one account of market exchanges and another of reciprocal ones. That cannot be right: if the class 'economic actions' or 'exchanges' does exist, it must be possible to make general statements about them. Admittedly, the possibility lies in the future; and so the second objection has some interim importance. And that is, that to establish the existence of a reciprocal type of economy (with its attendant economics) requires exactly the same procedures as marketists use to establish the underlying reality of profit motivation. Just as a marketist has to say that altruism is not really altruistic but is profit-motivated, so Sahlins has to say that – in a reciprocal economy – theft, for instance, is a form of reciprocity; together with market-like activity it is 'negative reciprocity'.

That term is a puzzle. Peoples do exist who exchange nasty things on a regular basis: in some pastoral communities, for instance, one group stands to another as mutual raiders – their relationship is that they steal from each other. And some accounts also suggest that feuding is a permanent relationship of homicidal threat (and occasional actual homicides). At a pinch, those could be called 'reciprocities', though to call them negative ones seems to refer to the nastiness of the things exchanged, which is an unusual foundation for a sociological or economic category. Or perhaps 'negative' refers to the intended balance sheet, to the hoped-for outcome of the exchange? Theft is certainly 'something for nothing', but a successful thief has a positive balance sheet, not a negative one, and hopes for no reciprocation at all. Trobrianders did not have formal relationships of the kind which pastoralist raiders and feuders had: their thieves and barterers were casual acquaintances, so far as one can tell. And in any case, the peoples who did have relationships of that kind also used them for other purposes – marriage is the prime example.

Theft and barter are as awkward to reciprocalist economists, as charity and altruism are to marketist ones; and what seems to be a similar (though scarcely elaborated) argument appears: these may not look like reciprocity, but the underlying reality is that they are.

So the reciprocalist argument is open to the same kind of objections, with the necessary changes of terms, which undermine the marketistic ones: the accounts are cooked somehow, to show perpetual balance or 'good measure'. In the case of buritila'ulo, for instance, Sahlins would have to show that the very careful calculation by Kakwaku villagers to make an exactly equal return was really the good measure they ostensibly tried to avoid for fear of warfare. Moreover, Sahlins's argument carries a further consequence, which is equally unwelcome. And that is that reciprocity is really confined to reciprocal economies – ones in which giving good measure is the dominant rule of exchange. Just as those, by definition, can have no market, so market-dominated societies can have no altruistic exchange, no reciprocity: it may seem to the natives of Britain or Canada that they do, but they are mistaken, and the underlying reality of those societies is very much as marketists describe it. But we know that the economists have got it wrong: our world is not so. And that puts us in a fix, because we know from Professor Sahlins that it isn't otherwise either.

The shared defects of marketist and reciprocalist arguments are two. The first is the assumption that under the surface of social activity lies a reality which is in some way truer or more real than mere appearances. In my experience it is indeed the case that reflection on appearances, and contemplation of them, can lead to understanding and even to explanation (of a provisionally satisfying kind): you think then of a 'deeper' reality. But it is unjustifiable to assume that what is deeper is necessarily more real. It cannot allow you to say, for example, 'My perception of the deeper reality shows that the natives' understanding is false; and that you can safely discount what they say': you cannot use evidence to build a model, and then use the model to discount the evidence. Secondly, these arguments are lopsided; they are partially deep. For clearly the profit motive (in a market) is part of the appearance, of the surface; and a marketist argument which says that the profit motive inspires blood donors therefore entails that it has a dual character: profit is the underlying reality of charity and alms; it is the surface of markets – but presumably underlies them too. Similarly, a reciprocalist account gives the reciprocity motive the double character of both overlay (as in kula) and underlay (as in buritila'ulo or theft). In both cases, in short, underlying reality does not always underlie but sometimes comes to the surface – like an outcrop of rock in a silted plain, or a cold current in a warm sea.

That is a defect because it is untidy: it is perfectly possible that at some point in the future someone will make a good theory of the relation between surface appearances and underlying reality – one which explains how some things can be both at once, and some can be one at one time and the other at another, while some things can only be surface phenomena. But that future has not yet arrived, and the untidiness seems now to be an arbitrary slipperiness, allowing marketists and reciprocalists to pass local native theories off as universal truths. What marketists have in fact done is to theorize about the market, on the surface of parts of their economies, and then extend their insights to those exchanges and economies which do not have significant markets nor a very widely accepted profit motive: in those cases, since the principles of market organization are not on the surface, they must be deeper – and more real. And so a theory which copes fairly well with market phenomena becomes transformed into the deep reality of all economic phenomena – without much to justify the extension, apart from confident ignorance. It is this extension, sometimes represented as hegemonic, that leads critics to suggest that those economists who concern themselves at all with non-market economic activities are overweening: they have taken a little local worst-case scenario, designed to cope with their local phenomena, and imposed it on the universe as a system of axioms. Reciprocalists fall into the same untidiness, even when their aim is to undermine marketistic economics.

The attack on the pretensions of market natives to explain everything was most clearly formulated by economic historians and marxist anthropologists from the 1940s. The marxists – most notable among them Godelier – had the advantage that they knew of a different underlying reality, and perceived that neo-classical economics was the OECD natives' justifying ideology for capitalism and economic imperialism. They knew that these phenomena, and the local theory which sustained them, were transitory stages in the march of progress. But it is not necessary now to be a marxist, to appreciate the strength of their local theory argument; and indeed marxism itself has come to have the character of another local theory.

In the nature of the case all theories are local, are natives' creations, because even a theory which in the event turns out to be general has to be created somewhere. Moreover, they must all aspire to being general, applicable to all cases in the category: it is difficult to imagine a theoretician settling down to say: 'I have no concern with anything other than the here and now, and shall rigorously exclude any general considerations'. So the criteria for choosing among theories are probably those of internal coherence, elegance and tidiness, and of closeness to the reality of individuals' motives and experience: it was Samuelson who argued against Friedman that, confronted with a number of alternative *as if* theories, a sensible person chooses the one which is closer to reality.

The marketist theory of exchange rests uneasily on a series of conjuring tricks in which the slipperiness of the concepts deceive the mind. The main anthropological alternative (that there are different types of economy identified by the dominant kind of exchange) shares some of those slipperinesses. Both deny the reality of natives' understandings of what they do; and both assert that 'reality' has a variable depth, can be both underlay and overlay.

I, too, wish to assert that there is an underlying pattern to exchange in all cultures. But I find it difficult to argue that it lies deeper in some instances than in others; and even more difficult to claim that it is more real than people's intentions and their statements about their actions.

3
Repertoires

So here is a project: to describe exchange in a way which accepts natives' experience that there are different kinds of exchange; and which explores an underlying reality which is so to speak consistently at the same level, and needs no claims made for it that it is more real than its overlay.

The range of kinds of exchange available to Britons or Trobrianders is the British (or Trobriand) repertoire. In ordinary speech a repertoire is the attribute of a class of individuals ('the repertoire for cellists') or of single members of the class ('he extended his repertoire to include the Bach suites'). Trombonists play only some of the pieces written for trombone, and consider the others too easy, or too difficult or too sentimental. But Trobrianders' personal exchange repertoires are restricted by social rank, gender and group membership rather than by skill and taste. Similarly in England many people are not thieves, rather few are employers and even fewer trade in commodity futures. This distribution of the British repertoire is similarly related to significant social differentiations of gender, age, wealth, social power, as well as aptitude and interest. However in this chapter the discussion of repertoire is chiefly concerned with the range of exchanges available to Trobrianders or Britons, rather than with the personal sense which the term also has.

The British repertoire, the 'list of all exchanges recognized by the natives of the British Isles', consists in the first instance of a list of words, as set out in Figure 1. This list excludes a large number of specialist terms, used for instance in the commodities markets, or in local marketplaces, or in academic language, and it does not have qualified terms (*wedding* present, *child* prostitution, *armed*

Figure 1 Part of the British repertoire

alms-giving	expropriation	reciprocity
altruism	extortion	renting
arbitrage	futures trading	retailing
banking	giving	robbery
barter	huckstering	scrounging
bribery	insider dealing	shoplifting
burglary	insurance	shopping
buying/selling	marketing	simony
charity	money-lending	social wage
commodity-dealing	mortgaging	swapping
corruption	mugging	theft
donation	pawning	tipping
employment	profiteering	trading
exploitation	prostitution	wholesaling

robbery): with all those it could extend to several pages. These words are intrinsically culture-bound. That is so with items such as simony, which identifies a (sinful) purchase of spiritual office in a Christian world. It is rather less obvious in the case of altruism (say) or reciprocity, which we attempt as English-speakers to elevate into a generally applicable category: people tend to regard these as something rather more seriously universal than insider dealing. It is quite true that you may identify words and actions in New Guinea or North Africa which you could reasonably translate as theft or alms-giving or whatever. However, people so often try to elevate their cherished local categories into universals, you might care to be on guard against the assumption that native British categories of exchange are more universal than they are. For instance, if you define altruism as an exchange which produces a particular kind of balance sheet (A makes losses, B makes gains) it is clear that altruism exists universally. That is because it is a logically possible outcome of any exchange: the same balance sheet could be produced from dishonest selling, for instance, or from ignorant shopping. And when I have been burgled, I do not consider I have been altruistic, even though I have made an absolute loss and the burglar has made a near-costless gain. In other words, Britons do not in fact define altruism simply by the kind of balance sheet it produces, and the intentions underlying the balance sheet are crucial. (It follows, incidentally, that it is very difficult for intention-less acts to be altruistic.) Altruism also involves, in Britain, a restricted kind of goods (some commodities are not really very suited to altruism), as well as a restricted range of relationships. So British altruism is complex; the more complex the notion, the less likely it is to turn out universal. The same argument applies to the various kinds of commercial transaction: they too are local natives' categories. We do indeed find things which look like them, and which we can quite unselfconsciously translate with 'arbitrage', 'shopping', 'prostitution'. But we too should be on our guard against tendencies to regard these as universal categories, and to erect a system of scientific laws on the basis of our local native understandings.

Each term in the British list refers to some different kind of exchange, and connotes a social world in which people evaluate not only goods and services, but also the relationship between the people concerned: the differences, in short, are essentially moral and legal and religious, as well as economic.

You can make a similar list for other social worlds. The Trobriand repertoire, attested in ethnographies over a period of 60 years or so, consists of some eighty named exchanges, and five or so other exchanges which Malinowski and his successors describe, but give no name to. These cover exchanges of labour, of specialized skills, of food during courtship and marriage and on various other formal and informal occasions; of clothing; gifts in return for sexual services; exchanges in anticipation of inheritance; the several exchanges associated with kula; and competitive and political exchanges such as buritila'ulo. It may be of interest to some readers to indicate the richly textured exchanges of Trobrianders by listing the sixteen distinct exchanges associated with marriage, as in Figure 2.

It seems fairly clear that the sixteen kinds of exchange associated with marriage engaged four kinds of people on each side and six kinds of commodity. In the pre-marriage exchanges (nos 61–9) the names of the exchanges identified a unique combination of person, commodity and direction. They were all exchanges in which the parties expected to achieve equality in a year or two: they were reciprocal. But once the marriage was established and recognized, the wife's brother had a generic obligation to supply his sister's husband with yams (70), and received in return a series of token valuables. The sources all state that in these exchanges the husband expected to come off best, and Malinowski in fact refers to him as receiving 'tribute'. These exchanges had different names, but involved the same commodities and people: they were all variations on the theme of *urigubu* further specified by an occasion – as it might be, an imminent *sagali* (77: not in the figure) or in the curious *likula bwayama* (74).

In short, each realized permutation of people and goods and occasion had its own name, indicating a categorizing system which tended towards the specific. That is a major difference between the Trobriand and the British repertoires. It does not imply a greater rigidity, since some of the names (urigubu in particular) had a wide semantic range, allowing people to shift senses and to exploit uncertain meanings: nevertheless, Trobrianders seem to have been really rather frequent labellers, even if their labels were sometimes ambiguous. Another major difference between the two repertoires is that Trobrianders often specified connections between exchanges. So, when a man received urigubu (70), he distributed a part of it to his close kinsmen and relatives to show he was held in respect: this was called *kovisi* (73, not in the figure). And the food he got as *vilakuria* (67) he distributed to the people who had helped him build his house (though Malinowski does not say whether that further distribution had a name). In short, many of the Trobriand exchanges are linked in a chain, with intriguing consequences. Of course, in Britain a wholesaler receives goods from a manufacturer, and then passes them on to a retailer; a professional earns a fee, and passes some of it on to the Inland Revenue. But my impression is that the Trobrianders were much more specific about this also. It is also the case that the relationships identified in the Trobriand repertoire were more durable and fixed than British ones: at any rate, more goods pass through those hands than do through the hands of people who are only casually associated, for a particular exchange.

A list of kinds of exchange is a series of distinctions: what makes a gift different from an act of charity is, first, that the gift-giver expects some return from the receiver but does not expect one for a charitable act. Second, the commodities which may be given as gifts (for example, jigsaw puzzles) are different from those which may be given as charity: toothbrushes and medicine, old clothes, basic foods could all be appropriate donations, would be inappropriate as

Figure 2 Summary of Trobriand marriage exchanges

Baskets of cooked yams

6 2 *Katuvila*: the parents' recognition of their daughter's marriage (Malinowski, 1929: 76; Weiner, 1976: 187).

6 3 1 basket of yams from each relative

Pepei: brought on the same day as *katuvila*. The groom's father distributes them to his kin, getting small valuables in return, which he uses for his eventual *takwelala pepei* [64] (Malinowski, 1929: 76).

6 4 Axe-blades and other small valuables

Takwelala pepei: 'a valuable returned for food'. He uses his relatives' valuables, some of his own, and sends them in the baskets which the *pepei* [63] came in (Malinowski, 1929: 77, 125).

6 5 1 'platter' of cooked food from each relative

Kaykaboma: recognition of the union, on the first day of cohabitation. Returned almost immediately with *mapula kaykaboma* [66] (Malinowski, 1929: 76).

6 6 1 'platter' of cooked food to each

Mapula kaykaboma: '(food) returned for food' (Malinowski, 1929: 76).

6 7 Large amounts of cooked food

Vilakuria: sent at the first harvest after the marriage. The husband distributes it to the people who helped build his house (Malinowski, 1929: 76–8; Weiner, 1976: 183).

6 8 Valuables

Takwelala vilakuria: (see also [64]). The two *takwelalas* should be about equivalent to all the first year's goods from the bride's family (Malinowski, 1929: 76,78).

6 9 Fish

Saykwala: a further return for *vilakuria* (Malinowski, 1929: 76,78).

Groom's parents

Bride's parents and relatives

Groom

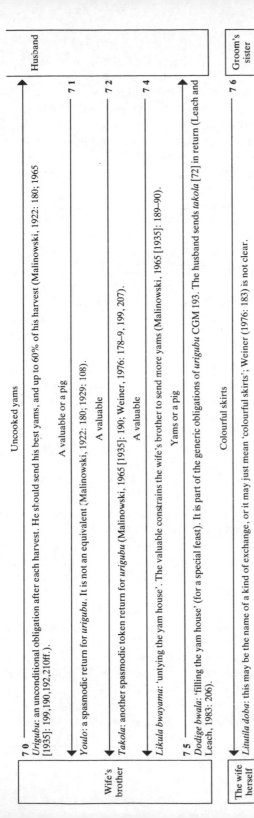

Husband

Uncooked yams

7 0
Urigubu: an unconditional obligation after each harvest. He should send his best yams, and up to 60% of his harvest (Malinowski, 1922: 180; 1965 [1935]: 199,190,192,210ff.).

A valuable or a pig

7 1
Youlo: a spasmodic return for *urigubu*. It is not an equivalent (Malinowski, 1922: 180; 1929: 108).

A valuable

7 2
Takola: another spasmodic token return for *urigubu* (Malinowski, 1965 [1935]: 190; Weiner, 1976: 178–9, 199, 207).

A valuable

7 4
Likula bwayama: 'untying the yam house'. The valuable constrains the wife's brother to send more yams (Malinowski, 1965 [1935]: 189–90).

Wife's brother

Yams or a pig

7 5
Dodige bwala: 'filling the yam house' (for a special feast). It is part of the generic obligations of *urigubu* CGM 193. The husband sends *takola* [72] in return (Leach and Leach, 1983: 206).

Colourful skirts

7 6
Litutila doba: this may be the name of a kind of exchange, or it may just mean 'colourful skirts'; Weiner (1976: 183) is not clear.

The wife herself

Groom's sister

Note. I have to admit that the procedure by which I have identified 'district' exchanges is open to question: Malinowski was not always very precise in identifying the parties to an exchange, and, for instance, could use 'bride's parents' and 'brides's father' interchangeably on different occasions (I have generally assimilated these persons). *Mapula* (food returned for food or a service) is generic, as is *takwelala* (valuable returned for food or a service); where the sources provide a qualifier (*takwelala pepei*) I have counted this as a distinct kind. But I agree that this is open to discussion.

A list of exchanges recorded in Trobriand ethnography is in preparation, using Hypercard 2.0 for the Apple Macintosh. It will be announced in due course.

(say) wedding presents. Third, the kinds of relationship are different: friends and family typically give presents; the wealthier typically provide charity for the poorer – though that is not invariably the case. You know, for instance, that poor people also experience compassionate movements of the heart, are moved to contribute to the relief of famine and earthquake. But poor people do not generally give to wealthy ones, and when the bereaved families of Aberfan became relatively wealthy because they had received so many donations it was clear that they were embarrassed. Some of the donors were cross: perhaps they thought charity should relieve poverty but not reverse it, and, seeing the objects of their benevolence become relatively wealthier, thought that they had been taken for a ride. You might say that when charity goes wrong we can perceive fairly clearly what people think charity should be, for on the whole people are more talkative about criteria when actions result in failure than they are about events which go off as they should.

What underlies these distinctions is that they are classifications – they match some things as fitting together, others as unfitting.

The earliest anthropological students of classification assumed that categories were related to each other in a hierarchy of generality, were taxonomies of the kind biologists use to classify animals and plants: so, there are a dozen or so species of larkspur; the larkspurs belong to the sub-class Helleboreae, which also includes the various species of globeflower, columbine, aconite. The Helleboreae belong to the Ranunculacaea, which also includes Paeonieae, Anemoneae. And so on. Each higher category is more inclusive, and the ultimate botanical category is 'Kingdom *Plantae*'. A diagram to represent a taxonomy looks like a family tree, showing a progressive specification of items.

Modern scholars point out that taxonomies (which are underwritten by assumptions about evolution) are not the only way in which categories can be related. Linguists coined the term partonomy to identify classificatory schemes in which the relation is between parts and whole, as in 'hand + foot + head + neck +. . . = body', or as in the British Registrar-General's 'A + B + C + D + E = society'. Some common categories in English usage are identified by their shared function, and have no more inclusive supercategory nor any identifiable lower-order items: 'toys' for instance is a category of 'things of any kind you can play with', and has no other unity than that given by the intention of the maker or user: dolls are generally toys for children, but they are also sold to tourists as souvenirs. Marbles were once bottle-stops, were then manufactured as toys, and are now sometimes used as ornaments. You can draw a generic tree, and other people can recognize it (saying perhaps 'That is a tree but I don't know what kind'): this is a crucial marker of a higher-level taxonomic category. You can't do the same with what Wierzbicka calls 'purely functional concepts': 'Draw me a toy' never results in a picture of which you could say 'Well I don't know what kind of toy it is, but it is clearly a toy'. The category toy exists, but it is not related taxonomically to marbles or tricycles (as tree is to oak or holly).

Another significant way in which people classify is by 'making twos' – pairing. This is the basis of Lévi-Straussian analysis of binary opposition. Lévi-Strauss claims that it underlies all human thought, but the more interesting proposition is the suggestion by Lancy and Strathern that pairing is an alternative to taxonomizing and to functional classifications. They argue that some people, most notably the Melpa of Mount Hagen in Papua New Guinea, pair more than they taxonomize; pairing can constitute a 'mind-set' quite distinct from the taxonomy-dominated thought processes of university students (people who confront masses of new information in a very short period, and who are typically the subjects of those experiments by cognitive psychologists which tend to show that taxonomizing is the *universally* most efficient mnemonic device). Pairs may be made of things which are similar, or different, complementary, allied, hostile, equal or alternative, and which have (as in the parent–child pair) all of these qualities as latencies. Pairing is very flexible also because each member of a pair can belong to other pairs: you can go on quite an extended tour of Kent, for instance, if you start at the Fox and Goose, and go on to the Fox and Hounds, then to the Hare and Hounds, and then to the Dog and Bear and to the Dog and Gun; the pairs cover the county.

In contrast to Melpa, I do not think Britons really have a pairing mind-set, although people do use pairing as one way of classifying among others: in particular for identifying relationships, which are infinitely transitive and are also complex because they combine hostility and complementarity, similarity, alliance, difference and alternation.

Lancy and Strathern argue that pairing (in its strong form as a mind-set) 'blocks' taxonomizing: the two are in some sense opposed, and they administered a series of test-tasks to Melpa which do tend to show that this is so. In Britain that obviously does not arise, but it is still the case that taxonomies are intrinsically hierarchical; they identify the plant and animal *kingdoms*, and attempt to put each item in its place. Even though all classificatory procedures are ambiguous and incomplete, pairs are intrinsically fluid and flexible, the associations are unstable and mobile. This leads to a Vichian speculation: in real kingdoms, pairs of real people are always potentially subversive of hierarchical order: you think not only of couples subverting the law and religion, but of pairs of green and experienced tax officials studied by Blau, the conspiracies between Tutor and Student against the College or University authorities, the complicities which develop between Customs Officer and Drug Smuggler.

However that may be, pairing is another form of classifying which is different from and perhaps opposed to taxonomies and functional methods of classifying. It is characteristically transitive, the items paired are mobile, and are complexly linked.

People use varied and overlapping procedures to classify things. In English law, for instance, the owner of a horse or a cow is not liable for damage it may cause when it strays. When a dog strays and causes a motor accident, is the owner liable? That depends on whether a dog is like a horse or a cow; and the relevant characteristics have been taken to be that it is indeed a domestic creature with a propensity to wander – hence horse-cow-like, hence creating no liability in owners. Systematic biologists use other criteria to classify dogs, and so do ordinary speakers of English. People can use different principles to classify the same thing in different groups at different times and that is one source of the flexibility and manipulability in classificatory activity.

People group items into categories and thus create mental order in the world. So the categories we create are social in the sense that we make them from within a social world. They are also social in the sense that the membership of a category, and the discontinuities between one category and another do not necessarily or essentially correspond to discontinuities or similarities in nature or logic; and they are social in the sense that they are sanctioned by human agencies. They are incomplete, imperfect, uncertain, open to negotiation and manipulation.

The starting point of this discussion was the question 'what underlies our perception and experience that there are kinds of exchange?' And my answer is a classification of intended exchange results, of commodities and of relationships, as set out in Table 3.

An intended exchange result (Figure 3) is a statement of the intended outcome of an exchange. For each of two people, income can be equal to outgo, more than outgo, or less than outgo (and in fact it can be a lot more, or just a little less). The intended exchange result is the desired or intended relation between A's balance and B's balance. In Figure 6 the axes are scales representing the balances (income less outgo) of two people, A and B. Any exchange result can be plotted on the graph as a point in relation to both scales.

So E1 is an exchange in which each person intends that they should each have a positive balance of (say) 15 units. In E2 they intend that A should have a negative balance, and B a positive one. In E3 they both strive to achieve zero balances. These points on the scale only have meaning in relation to the intentions of A and B: so E1 could be perfect commerce: each party makes a satisfactory

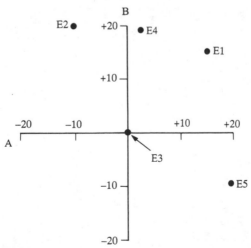

Figure 3   Intended exchange results

Table 3 Kinds of exchange

Intended result	Commodity	Relationship
For each exchange partner:	Books Food Drink	Kin Husband ↔ Wife Parent ↔ Child Uncle ↔ Niece etc.
(a) Income < Outgo	Sex Pork-belly futures Money Toothbrushes	Pretend kin Godparent ↔ Godchild Aunt ↔ 'Nephew'
(b) Income > Outgo	Blood Labour Generators Trobriand armshell or necklace	Lover ↔ Lover Buyer ↔ Seller Patron ↔ Client Teacher ↔ Pupil
(c) Income = Outgo	Uncooked yams Tobacco	Friend ↔ Friend Judge ↔ Plaintiff Doctor ↔ Nurse
(i.e nine possible combinations)	Betel Clothes etc.	Doctor ↔ Patient Employer ↔ Employee etc.

A kind of exchange is composed of an intended exchange result, and a commodity, and a relationship. Any combination may be appropriate or not.

profit, they are pleased with themselves and with each other. E2 could be the result desired when A sets out to be altruistic, E3 when they are planning a bit of reciprocity. The aim is the essential element, since the result itself tells us nothing: E5 or E2 could be failed reciprocity; and if A is a shopper, B a shopkeeper, E4 is profiteering, and E3 a really rather unsatisfactory commercial endeavour. Results only have meaning in relation to the intentions of the exchangers, which they generally frame in terms of a named kind of exchange, between people in an identified social relationship, using appropriate commodities.

Income and outgo are composites, sums of a range of items which are socially defined as relevant. The relevant items are different for different kinds of exchange, they are different in different countries, they change in the course of time, and they may be asymmetric (you do not always assess my costs in the way I do). So, although gift-receivers may notice and appreciate that the giver has been to a lot of trouble to provide a particular gift, neither person is generally so scrupulous in their accounting as shopkeepers are, for shopkeepers include transport, warehousing, conservation and display in their accounts. Similarly, when you plan to send a hundred Christmas cards, you may calculate the time and postage required, but you do not include these costs in your receipts: you welcome each separate card as a token of goodwill and of continuing friendship, and do not say, as it might be, 'they only send 50 cards and so could have afforded something better': the accounting is asymmetric. In Britain the accounting procedures for public bodies such as universities are rather different from those of commercial firms; and internationally it is scarcely surprising that the accounting procedures which are accepted as giving a true and fair view of an Egyptian company are different from those used for American or French ones. These remarks serve to show that the elements which compose 'income' and 'outgo' are socially defined partonomies, depending on local criteria of relevance: they are not scientific or objective.

In many British exchanges, and in most Trobriand ones, exchangers intend that the result should be significant on both scales – that is to say, A is concerned with B's result as well as his own, and vice versa. In a shop I am assumed to be able to work out what it is that I want more than I want my money. And while I have some guarantee that the food is not rotten, the electric cable is safe, the second-hand car will go, it is not the shopkeeper's job to decide whether I like the taste of beans, or have the right gauge cable for the current I shall put through it, or mightn't prefer a faster car of a different colour. Those matters are my business: the rule *caveat emptor* applies, and each party to a commercial exchange is expected to look out for their own interest. But that is not so for all exchanges: when you give gifts you are expected to consider the welfare and interests of the person you are giving to. To give a book to someone who does not read is mildly insulting, whatever the commercial value of the present. If someone needs bread, you do not generally give him a stone, although it has happened that aid-givers have sent their surplus snow-ploughs to tropical countries. Contemporary development experts who discuss issues of appropriate technology are concerned with what commodities are truly more valuable to aid-receiving countries, and with how to persuade prestige-conscious Ministers of Development that a thousand methane-powered generators are more truly useful than a single nuclear power station. The rule *caveat emptor* – look out for your own utility – contrasts with the rule 'Do not look a gift-horse in the mouth': you have a right to expect that someone who is giving you a horse has your welfare at heart, and so you should not look under the bonnet to check that it is in running order; at any rate, not while the giver is still around. We expect that givers put themselves in our shoes, and that they should try to calculate our utility. It is not a matter of calculating the true or objective value, but of imagining someone else's evaluation: in jargon, it involves inter-subjectivity.

The importance of this second element is such that people sometimes class exchanges by it alone: commerce, insurance, employment are all daylight robbery; gift-giving, charity and the donation of blood are all altruistic. This is significant in people's aspirations and creativity because they argue about the justice and niceness of economies, and have preferences for kinds of economy. But it is clear that in practice they do distinguish also by the proper relations between income and outgo. Gifts between friends should more or less balance; gifts exchanged between parents and children should be unequal. Altruists should expect no return, while alms-givers may quite legitimately hope for a supernatural reward. All these are different appropriate relations between income and outgo, even though in each case givers are expected to put themselves in the other person's shoes. Similarly, shopkeepers expect and are expected to make a reasonable profit, but a good burglar gets astounding returns for a minimal outlay – even though both shopkeepers and burglars are concerned with their own utilities.

In summary, an intended exchange result is a balance of two partonomies together with an expectation in some cases that the parties try to assess the other's utilities as well as their own.

If you present a toothbrush to a friend as a birthday gift you behave unconventionally, as you do if you offer to buy a public office for cash. In practice Britons work with categories which are fairly clear, that identify which commodities are suitable for gifts, for commerce, or for charity. The categories overlap: many things can be bought or given without offence; and indeed, we buy many things – cards, books – which we then later give away. Manufacturers are aware of this and sometimes provide special gift wrappings for mundane objects; or they use Christmas or wedding seasons to introduce special kinds of new goods. People buy some things only for giving away: I think it is true that most people would mock someone who bought Christmas cards to put on their own mantelpiece. And other things such as floorcloths are bought but are generally not given: you might in an emergency beg one from a neighbour, but if he gave you an unsolicited one for your birthday, you might reasonably consider your position. In general however, the categories buyable and giveable overlap each other to a considerable extent; and manufacturers know that.

The category commodity at a common-sense level consists of material objects – toothbrush, potato, Christmas card. At a more complex level, the thing may be an abstraction – labour power, a concert performance, the protection offered by a government or a mafia. Some scholars say that people exchange reputation, 'name'; they are probably right and, if so, that is a thing of this kind. Commodities may also be abstracted rights: a warrant entitles the owner to purchase shares at a named price before some date in the future; and people deal in commodity futures. Clearly commodities are not natural objects, but invented ones: what may be a commodity varies from society to society, and from time to time. For instance, at any rate in East Kent, people now all generally agree that for many purposes people are not commodities, although their predecessors in that territory used to include slave-owners and slave-exchangers. So, some physical, material entities are socially defined as not things – not exchangeable.

The category commodity is defined by function: it is like the category toys, and is a subset of 'all things' distinguished by the judgement that they are exchangeable. We subdivide the category 'exchangeable things': some are good for selling, others for giving, others for both. All these, like 'good for giving at Christmas', 'good for eating *en famille*', 'good for eating with guests' are identified by their function – the purposes we put things to. 'It was not a dinner to ask a man to', Dr Johnson said to Mrs Thrale after one of her suppers; and although you would never be so blunt, you understand exactly what he meant. The things we put in these categories can – like dogs – be classed in other ways. Azaleas have their taxonomic place in the Kingdom *Plantae*; and they are also citizens of the functionally defined Republic *Thingi*, where florists sell them as ideal presents for Christmas.

The relationship of the people who exchange affects what sort of intended result is appropriate: parents and children, for instance, aim at different results from shoppers and shopkeepers, or teachers and pupils. So kinsmen do not usually make commercial exchanges, or when they do they may ask or offer special terms. People generally expect parents to make losses on their exchanges with their children (and, an additional complication, to treat their children equally). Teachers and their pupils are in the same position within the much more restricted exchanges between them; and so are givers of charity, and altruists. Friends expect to make equal exchanges (considering the other's utility); and it has been said that, in England, people who are approaching friendship and begin to exchange gifts tend to give at birthdays, or as an occasional gift, rather than at Christmas. The tactic is clear: Christmas gifts are simultaneous, or nearly so, and allow little time for the gift receivers (who can find themselves unexpectedly in that role) to match the gift received. On the other hand, birthdays and other personal occasions are usually spaced, allowing the receivers time to make the necessary judgements and assessments. Commercial exchanges are also 'equal', in the sense that each person gets what they want; but they do not match utility, and shopkeepers or bankers or industrialists are more or less indifferent to each single customer. It is true that meeting a market or creating one does imply some judgement about what other people want. But to say 'there is a market for mousetraps', or 'there could be a market for zloty futures', is not the same, in terms of motive and intention, as saying 'I shall knit a really long football scarf for Peter's birthday'. Theft is stereotypically anonymous, and although thieves may in fact be known as friends, children, employees, they hope that they will never be uncovered as thieves and forced to make a return for what they have taken. Altruists also often act by stealth: anonymous benefactors clearly expect no earthly return for what they have given. Blood donors positively hope they will never be on the receiving end of the tube, though they may have that possibility in mind when they give their blood. But even when the parties are known to each other, the suggestion that there should be some return other than thanks, recognition that the donor has done well, is inappropriate. Charity is its own reward, in the sense that the donor has the intention of saving his soul: God rewards alms-giving, Allah rewards zakat. No human hand need make a return.

Our classes of people are usually paired: mother and child; seller and buyer; teacher and student; (pork belly future) trader and (pork belly future) trader; kula partner and kula partner. When the people are corporate groups (buritila'ulo village and buritila'ulo village; wife-givers and wife-takers; shareholders and takeover bidder) they also seem to be classed by the principle of 'making twos' analysed by Lancy and Strathern. Even when a shopkeeper has more than one customer, or a teacher more than one student, people think of it as a series of one-to-one relationships which together create the business or the school. Some of these relationships last longer than others: parents and children are in a more stable relationship that shopkeepers and customers. The duration of the relationship does often correspond (as Sahlins has emphatically noted) with the kind of intended exchange result which exchangers hope to achieve; and although shopkeepers or manufacturers may sometimes wish that they had stable relations with their customers, they have to tread carefully: customers who become friends may expect favoured treatment, extended credit and even cancellation of debts. Another variation among the pairs concerns relative power: mothers are generally more powerful vis-à-vis their children than kula-ists are vis-à-vis their partners. This is partly a matter of law; it may also be because one party to the exchange is more indifferent than the other (this is the basis of Blau's ingenious arguments, mentioned below in Chapter 6). But it is not the case that greater power always results in exploitation, although in some classic cases it does (see, for instance, the discussion of patrons and clients in Chapter 5 below).

In conclusion, a kind of exchange is itself a partonomy made out of paired relationships, of functionally classified commodities and of desired balances between two sets of income and outgo (which are themselves partonomies). It is this categorization which underlies exchanges rather than a particular motive or automatic working out of natural laws. I have argued that one defect of marketistic accounts of exchange is that the universal profit motive is said to underlie charity or reciprocity, but is on the surface of market exchanges. That dual character – both overlay and underlay – is intellectually messy, and does not convey the richness of our own experience as exchangers. I think that this account, arguing that what underlies exchanges is a morally, legally and ritually sanctioned classification scheme, does not share that untidiness. Another defect of marketistic arguments is that the model of exchange has to be more real than the understanding and experience of exchangers. You may agree that as a shopper you are indeed market-oriented and profit-motivated, but argue that as a mother you have no thought of profit when you care for your children. A marketist is compelled to say that your mothering is none the less profit-motivated: you may not be aware of it, but there is an income in it for you somewhere – in the prestige you gain among mothers, in the future care your children will provide when you are old and decrepit. In short, marketists are bound to argue that you deceive yourself and that their model is more real than what you understand.

The classificatory model of exchanges is a model, a construct, like a marketist's. But it never requires you to claim that it is more real than experience. And if an informant tells you that there is a kind of exchange you had not thought of, you do not have to say he must be mistaken, you simply add it to the list, another item in the repertoire.

The model I propose is therefore clean, at least on these two counts. Is it useful? I shall argue in the next chapters that it does explain differences between economies more satisfactorily than its chief rival: that is, because it takes as central these moral and religious and legal distinctions which all people make among kinds of exchange and which marketists have to relegate to the periphery of their vision, classifying them as imperfections. On the other hand, it is not particularly useful as a guide to intervention or planning by state's men. That is mainly because it is so positivist: it is very difficult to convert it from a model into a goal. One of the attractions of the marketists' model of perfect competition is that however unreal and unclean it may be as a model, it is very easy to take it as a description of how the world ought to be, as a set of conditions we should try to achieve.

Another defect of the classificatory model, from a predictive or political economist's point of view, is that its classifications are not fixed and rigid but are social playthings, one of the major areas of human invention and inconsistency. For we constantly exploit the ambiguities and uncertainties of the mental structures we superimpose on unruly social worlds: classifications, and particularly classifications of exchanges, are extremely unstable fields of action, open to manipulation, fixing, deceit – to all sorts of creative and interested chicanery and goodwill. In market exchanges generally this is well known. But it is also true of charitable activities, for instance when people try to pass self-interested actions as altruistic. Some of the most entertaining and successful confidence tricks have been those which exploited the benevolence and goodwill of the marks rather than their greed.

In short, one of the points of a classificatory model is that it incorporates fluidity and ambiguity as well as creative manipulation, not as failures of an intellectual system, but as part of its essence. That is not good for governments, which are on the receiving end as often as they are on the manipulating end; and consequently it is not much use either to the state's men-political economists whose importance derives from their ability to give clear and simple advice, based on a system of natural law.

A repertoire is a set of pieces which a population may play. They are not all equally available to each person, partly as a result of the exercise of social power. But in general people do seem to think that exclusive or excessive devotion to only one or only a few kinds of exchange is reprehensible. In Britain we certainly think that a purely altruistic person is as unbalanced as someone who is only interested in commerce. A blood donor who donates all his blood is clearly mad. And in fact we reserve respect and public honours for successful shopkeepers and industrialists who are notably active in other kinds of exchange as well. Even at a less exalted level we expect people to engage in a range of activities, and to be as successful in domestic exchanges as in their market ones. Like Trobrianders, we have a notion of what a man or woman ought to do if they are to lead a full and reasonable life. A Trobriand man who wished to be considered good of his kind had to participate in urigubu and *youlo*, in kula and kovisi, and to do so fairly and honestly with some success. We expect our acquaintances to try to be rounded people with a reasonable personal repertoire: then we may call them good of their kind – good men, good women, good shopkeepers, good Registrars. In my view it is this image of what a whole person is, and the desire to be considered good of one's kind, that leads us to try to be market-wise in commerce, reciprocal with our friends, a little bit charitable, and altruistic up to a point. It is not, in other words, a profit motive (now open, now concealed, now buried so deep we deny its existence) which impels us to engage in exchange. It is rather the notion we have of what a full life and a whole rounded person should be that leads us to attempt to play a number of different pieces from the repertoire available.

Consequences

The notion of exchange is a composite classification, and the force which underpins it is not any kind of natural law, but the social force of morals, laws, governments and the human agents of divine authority. These constraints are much less constraining than gravity is, or thermodynamics, and consequently exchange activity contains manipulation, instability and complexity. One of the problems which flows from that position concerns the performance of economies. I am rather too aware that I cannot deal with it as well as I would wish. I sometimes imagine what a wholly irrefutable account of my position would look like; and then measure up the kind of demonstration I can in fact produce. The discrepancy is rather frightening, and if I continue that is because I can also measure up other people's arguments against the standard, and find that they too are unsatisfactory.

The point is really rather simple: does the notion of an exchange repertoire add anything to what we can say about economies? At one level it obviously does, since it enables us to integrate the meanings which people attribute to their actions, to investigate their affective responses to others, and to explain the interconnections among economy, politics, religion, morality, kinship. I think that this would be agreed – it is at least one way of approaching these matters; and they are important to the people who choose to act in one way rather than another. I think something of the kind would be conceded by most students of economics, of whatever persuasion. For instance, recent economic reforms in Britain and the European Community are discussed not simply as technical matters, but as ones involving issues of great political importance. And even campaigns for greater efficiency in business or the provision of health care are argued as moral issues, with the underlying assumption that it is significantly immoral to waste scarce resources on frivolous or ill-considered purposes. The passions which those discussions arouse clearly indicate that they are not simply technical and therefore morally or politically neutral and unprovoking. We argue about how we should organize our economies, we consider some preferable to others, we fantasize about ideal economic systems just as much as we do about politics, and almost as much as we do about sex and intellectual matters.

We can gain subtlety if we can integrate these meanings into the analysis of exchange. But subtlety entails complexity, and one of the attributed virtues of marketist analysis is its simplicity and elegance: marketism works well enough, it is said, for what it is supposed to do, which is no more than to predict and control markets in a rough and ready sort of way. The main assumption underlying 'other things being equal' is that for those purposes it doesn't matter very much if things are different, since they all boil down to the same thing, more or less; and marketists can safely reach for their silencers when they hear the word 'culture', or when an anthropologist mentions meanings or symbolism.

We can be as sensitive and scrupulous as we choose about meanings and symbols, but if they have no consequences, or none we can demonstrate, we will be fairly unconvincing. We have to show that different politics, morals, religions and aesthetics have identifiable consequences for exchange.

Unfortunately we have not got very much evidence that helps in the task. Anthropologists have often been content to note that natives' actions and their principles and organization of exchange are exotic, leaving the field open to those who wish to talk about imperfections. It is also true that it is very difficult to measure the economy of a tribe or an island, and to collect the statistics which might show that an economy based on non-market principles of integration performs differently. Blue Books, for all their conventional inadequacies, are a boon when you want to make an informed guess about long-term trends in an economy. Moreover, when an entire economy produces say one new canoe every couple of years, you can begin to wonder whether statistics would mean anything, and indeed whether industrial output is an appropriate measure for activities which are (you wish to argue) based on different principles.

The person who has contributed most to the study of the performance of non-OECD economies if Professor Sahlins. He considers the issue of exchange value: when people exchange goods in non-market economies, how do they set the rate? Do those rates then change, and if so how and why? He discusses five cases of trade where we know something of the exchange rates and something about how they change, and his conclusion is that the rates are fixed in the short term; that in the longer term they shift to accommodate changes in supply or demand; and that in each case the trade is between exclusive partners, that is, it is a closed system. He goes on to make the point that this is a remarkable combination of factors. For in orthodox economics what is supposed to make prices change is competition in a market. Supply and demand meet in a market, prices shift up or down to reach the level at which all the pigs are sold, all the pots disposed of, because buyers and sellers are in competition among themselves. The curious thing, therefore, is that in this trade there is no competition: the motive force for price fluctuations is missing. In general terms this is a problem because it suggests that the iron laws of economics are not so iron as all that: if price fluctuations can be the result of more than one cause, the marketists' explanation looks rather less than conclusive.

That is an interesting result, but not much help if you want to show that differences in moral order produce different results; to find that – give or take a few variations, such as the speed of response – they produce the same or similar results is disappointing. A further possibility is the OECD economies. They produce statistics, and they have multi-principled economies. The statistics might show the effects of different principles, so that we could have some circumstantial evidence for differential effects of the parts of the repertoire.

It was estimated that the value of gifts which were bought in the marketplace in the late 1960s in Britain and then given away was a little more than £1 billion a year. That was 4.3 per cent of all consumer expenditure. And it was a conservative estimate, based only on those commodities for which there were market research reports. Many goods were not covered; and, of course, there was no accounting for home-produced goods – knitted scarves and home-made Christmas cards – which do not appear in the national accounts. Nor was there any possibility of estimating the exchange of lunch and tea and dinner parties. The relatively hard figure of £1

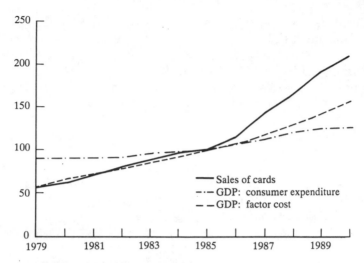

Sources: for sales of cards: *Keynote Report,*
Greetings Cards, 4th edn 1985; 7th edn 1991;
for GDP:
Central Statistical Office, *United Kingdom*
National Accounts (Blue Book), 1991 edn.
London: HMSO, Table 1.7.

Figure 4 Indices for sales of greetings cards and GDP, UK, 1979–90
(1985 = 100)

billion could rise quite considerably, if we were able to include all
reciprocities, to something like 7–8 per cent of consumer expenditure. These figures suggest that there is a sizeable part of the British
economy which is dedicated to producing gifts; and there is some
very slender evidence which suggests that that part of the economy
performs differently from the parts which do not. In periods of
recession the demand for machine-tools declines, as do most
industries which supply industrial equipment, the building trade,
motor manufacturers and ordinary household goods such as
washing machines, brooms, fridges. But it seems possible that those
industries which produce a high proportion of gift goods (things
which are bought and then given on) do not show the same effect:
sales of toys, games, jewellery, greetings cards and aftershave
seemed to remain fairly immune to recession, at any rate in the
years around 1970.

But that evidence is very slender, based on journalists' reports of how people seemed to be spending their money in periods of economic difficulty. Is it possible to produce a long-term series of figures to establish that the gift producers' performance is different from the general trend of the industrial economy?

Figure 4 shows the indices for retail sales of greetings cards (current market prices) in the UK for an eleven-year period, and compares them with factor cost GDP and consumer expenditure. You cannot doubt that in that period sales of cards did not follow, match or mimic changes in the conventional measures of the economy; but two questions follow. Can you take greetings cards to represent the general run of gift goods? The answer is a very cautious 'maybe'. Retailing strategies for cards have changed in ways which were not open to retailers of other gift goods. For instance, in the 1960s and 1970s, the invention and diffusion of charity cards might explain unusual performance by the industry: manufacturers made cards with the charity's name on them, and when a donor bought cards he made a contribution to the charity, sending the receipts to his friends and relatives. That increased the market in ways which are not open to manufacturers of tricycles or hair-driers, and might explain the growth in sales at that time. A more recent development has been the increase in the number of specialist shops, in imitation of florists and of the (generally rather unsuccessful) dedicated toyshops of the 1960s. Market reports also suggest that households have become smaller and kin more scattered in the last decades, and that cards therefore satisfy a need for dispersed and inarticulate members of families to communicate standardized sentiments on formal occasions. In fact the range of cards has increased, and so have the types of pre-printed message: the new cards are more expensive than Christmas cards, so that the increase in numbers of cards sold is less than the increase in cash paid by customers. For all these reasons, it is wise to be very cautious before assuming that sales of cards represent a general trend in reciprocities.

The second question is, can you use the graph to support the argument that that part of the economy which is integrated by the reciprocity motive performs differently from the part which is integrated by the profit motive? And here again the answer is 'maybe'. For if sales of cards are not representative, conclusions drawn are doubtful. Nevertheless, you would have to explain why the marketers' ingenuity has been so successful – better than the

going rate for other manufacturers and retailers. You might say that
they have created a demand out of the blue, something which did
not exist before. Or you might say that they have enhanced and
nurtured tendencies which were already present in the purchasing
population. It is certainly an interesting hypothesis that the natives
of Britain make judgements about gift purchases which are
different from those they make about consumption purchases; and
that might be because while people can go without a meal, or eat
more cheaply, or forgo some useful good such as a washing machine
for a while, they cannot suspend friendship or kinship or clientship
for the interim: people do not interrupt social relationships in a
recession and then resume them when times get better. It is much
easier to interrupt direct consumption.

   The actions of manufacturers also lend some support to this
circumstantial case. It is quite clear that they adapt their production
and marketing strategies to take account of Britons' propensity to
purchase goods and then give them away. That is manifest in their
statements and their practice. So, for instance, florists and manufacturers of greetings cards and of men's cosmetics suffered (in the
1960s and 1970s) from marked seasonality of sales: that is inconve-
nient to manufacturers because they have to run their plant and
employ their staff for the whole year, while their income is rather
lumpy and intermittent. They could have done other things:
diversified into other products, for example, which were not
seasonal. But what they did in fact was to try to create other
occasions for giving: Mother's Day – itself a relatively recent
elaboration of the Christian Mothering Sunday – was matched with
Father's Day a few months later; and there was also a move to
establish Grandmother's Day in another period of the year. In
short, the strategy was not to encourage people to consume directly,
and so to create an evenly spaced demand, but to get them to give
gifts more often, at intervals throughout the year.

   Another strategy was adopted by some manufacturers who did
not produce gift goods. It is very striking that the big manufacturers
of industrial and of 'white' goods (fridges, washing machines,
driers) set up lines of production for smaller items such as
hair-driers, toasters, coffee- and tea-makers. These are all items
which are given – often as wedding presents – and the manufacturers diversified into these goods in order to counterbalance
fluctuations in demand for non-gift goods. That is to say, they

certainly thought that people's propensity to give was independent
to some extent of their propensity to consume, and consequently
they could produce gifts as a hedge against fluctuations in their main
market.

I find this significant and supportive; and when I hear people
complaining about 'the commercialization of Christmas' I am rather
pleased since it seems to me that it could be put the other way
round: it could be an instance of the gifting of the market, and could
be a demonstration of the instability of markets relative to the
continuing strength of gift-giving. However, this evidence, pleasing
as it is, is circumstantial and not conclusive. Nevertheless, when you
see that a shop is selling a new kind of attachment to DIY drills,
packaged in boxes decorated with holly; or when you see an
advertisement that suggests goods are ideal for gifts, you might
consider the possibility that manufacturers, like anthropologists,
know more about the motives for exchange than marketist economists do.

The evidence is circumstantial, and not enough to convict a felon
with. But what it suggests is that when you can collect figures
covering long periods of time you may be able to discern hints that
different kinds of exchange have different consequences for the
performance of economies. That is of course not news to marketists, who have to explain differences in terms of the varying impact
of imperfection. But it is perhaps useful to show that the perceptions of ordinary natives (who know that there are different kinds of
economy, and argue about which they prefer) correspond to real
differences in performance; and to do so with a model which takes
the political, moral, legal aspects of exchange to be central.

Manipulators and Controllers

Social classifications are not fixed. That is partly because they are inherently incomplete, partly because they are ambiguous. So on the one hand, the constructions of the mind can never account for all the variety of the world. And on the other, the criteria we create to decide which things belong together are never sufficiently precise or permanent to make every allocation certain. That is true of scientific taxonomies of plants, which are continually revised. It is even more true of insubstantial items such as exchanges: they are complex categories, and they involve commodities, balance sheets and above all people – all of which are categorized. People have multiple roles, mixed motives and capacities for concealment, deception and self-deception which are denied to vegetables.

The generic term for things which do not fit into a category at all, or which fit in more than one, is anomaly. And some anthropologists, most notably Douglas, have emphasized the awkwardness which anomalies create in the minds of classifiers: they are abominations, as in Leviticus, and people treat them with special reverence or horror or avoidance. That may be so in some cases. But in many others, the imperfection of classes may be an opportunity, giving people room for manoeuvre, scope for inventiveness and creativity. Ambiguity and uncertainty surely can be disturbing; but they also allow people to play, do not necessarily constrain them to pray.

As an example, consider Trobriand urigubu. In its core meaning it is an annual exchange of yams from a wife's brother to his sister and her husband, and the return is an optional occasional token of much less value. By keeping the relationship nourished with urigubu a man expected eventually to be able to assert his claim to his sister's children, but even so Malinowski refers to urigubu as a sort of tribute, and later writers have not denied that it connotes inferiority and dependence.

In 1918 the Trobriand village of Omarakana had been in turmoil for various reasons, and the chief (as Malinowski calls him) decided to try to restore some prestige and harmony by organizing a magnificent display of wealth. In spite of a bad harvest he called on the villagers to give him tribute in recognition of his political authority and as a sign that they were united behind him. 'Chief' was neither a very powerful nor fully recognized office in the Trobriands. Malinowski, according to later anthropologists who worked there, exaggerated the formality of a leader's position, which was more achieved than ascribed, and which required continuous negotiation and maintenance. People knew of 'tribute', but did not pay it as a matter of course. In 1918 seventy-seven villagers responded to the chief's call and delivered rather more than 20,000 baskets of yams, a rather impressive quantity. But of the seventy-seven, only two men called their contribution tribute. Most of the others called it urigubu.

Chiefs were polygynous, and so thirty-five of the contributors had some connection through his wives, as wife's brother or other fairly close kinsman. Their contribution was urigubu in one of the stricter senses of the term. The remaining forty men, faced with a demand to acknowledge political dominance, passed their tribute as urigubu. They were not close kinsmen of any of his wives, but stretched their genealogical definitions so that their relationship to the chief became one in which urigubu became proper and appropriate.

Urigubu certainly connoted a 'tributary relationship' and acknowledged dependence, but it was not tribute: it implied kinship and future expectation, and people who gave urigubu as an alternative to tribute were able to meet the demands of their chief without acknowledging his claims as a holder of political office. The chief got his yams, he made his grand display, and he seemed to vindicate his claim to the produce of the village. You can imagine that all parties were more or less satisfied, and that they achieved this by exploiting the ambiguities of categories: the same action meant different things to different people, and in 1918 they avoided conflict by tacitly accepting that the chief and commoners interpreted the harvest levy in different ways. That is I think a case of

complicit exploitation of what Herzfeld in another context calls
disemia, a kind of cultural pun which allows people to get along
provided they do not have to acknowledge that they use the one
word but give it different meanings. G. Lienhardt uses parallax to
similar effect: in studies of politics and religion it is clearly necessary
to incorporate notions of peace-creating misunderstanding; and it
seems to me that the chief of Omarakana's harvest of 1918 was
another case, in economy.

That play on categories was an either-or: either tribute or marriage exchange. Clearly there are other ways in which people can
play with categories: puns are not the only game, but it is not in fact
very easy to find examples of fundamental manipulations. That is
because anthropologists have tended to regard anomalies as serious
and frightening (to natives); and economists to think of them as imperfections. So it may be worth summarizing one economist's account of involuntary unemployment because it seems that he may
have identified a very widespread additive category-game.

The problem Akerlof addresses is that neo-classical economists
have got no satisfactory explanation of involuntary unemployment:
if the number of people wishing to sell labour is greater than the
demand, then the price at which labourers are prepared to sell
should fall to a level at which employers will buy, and the market
should clear. The fact that this doesn't happen and that for instance
employers buy labour from expensive white adults when they could
strike deals with much cheaper black adolescents, is hard to explain
in orthodox neo-classical economics. Of course, the distribution of
skills in a population of labourers is an issue; and so is the provision
of welfare payments for the unemployed and the demand for the
employers' products. But neither of these accounts for the levels of
involuntary unemployment, nor for the way in which it is cheap
labourers who are mainly unemployed.

Akerlof's solution is to say that 'a fair day's wage for a fair day's
work' is more than a simple market bargain. The notions of fairness
are more than a marketist price since they involve more than the
going rate of wage, more than the going rate of work. So Akerlof
suggests that on top of, in addition to, the market bargain,
employers and employees exchange gifts which create solidarities
and understandings between all parties. 'On the workers' side, the
"gift" given is work in excess of the minimum work standard; and on
the firm's side the "gift" given is wages in excess of' the market rate.

So the women clerical workers whose effort Akerlof discusses, worked on average 18 per cent harder than the firm's norm; and the firm treated the workers 'fairly'. Each party gave good measure. Akerlof's account is not entirely convincing. Apart from the irony that his source of sociological data is the work of G. C. Homans, the sociologist who is best known for his attempts to introduce a neo-classical exchange theory into sociological analysis, Akerlof's intention is to make gift giving part of the calculation of utilities: if you can get a job and exchange gifts with your employer, your utility is increased. That is not a very bold departure from the orthodoxies of marketist analysis, since it does not increase the number of integrating motivations in play: it is more timid, for instance, than related discussions of morality and justice in exchange by Sen. Moreover, Akerlof's identifcation of the component of fairness as a 'gift exchange' is uneasy: you may doubt that any of the parties would have put it quite like that, and wonder if Akerlof thinks he has discovered an underlying reality.

In spite of the rather large element of 'as if it were a gift', Akerlof's discussion is stimulating and suggestive. We know from experience and from nearly all the studies by sociologists of work that employment is not simply a market relationship: employers hope for commitment and dedication from workers who in turn expect recognition and support. Labour power is not a commodity which can be detached from a person and bought or sold like dry goods, even though we may sometimes choose to think of it in that way. It is an intimate part of the person, used to provide a personal service; and contracts which involve it ideally engage self-respect as well as the profit motive. In the Protestant ethic work is a religious as well as an economic necessity; and even though many jobs can hardly be said to engage the full spirituality of workers, the notion that work is essential for the well-being of a whole person underlies our concern about unemployment, and about the changing character of work in contemporary Britain. It is precisely the non-marketable sociability of employment, the extra commitment, which allows organizations to function: it was after all Blau (another marketistic exchange theorist) who demonstrated that an ideal-typical Weberian rational bureaucracy could not possibly 'work' unless it were suffused with the sociabilities of give and take within the informal hierarchies of the workplace.

So to that extent at least Akerlof's analysis of the gift of fairness in employment is convincing: you may hesitate to call it a gift; you may regret that he wishes to include gift giving in the calculus of utilities; nevertheless it certainly seems to be the case that the exchanges between employers and employees are a package of different types of exchange. It is that complexity of the exchanges which appears to be associated at any rate in part with 'good' labour relations, and it is a manifestly creative use of the categories of exchange.

The disemic complexity of the chief of Omarakana's urigubu was created by villagers who in effect said 'we give you yams as brothers-in-law and not as subjects': they manipulated the relationship component of the exchange by substituting one relationship with another. Akerlof argues that in fair employment the parties manipulate the terms of exchange: in addition to the rational profit-motivated primary contract, the workers offered more, on other terms (which he wants to call reciprocal); it is additional. These are quite subtle manipulations, and the attraction of the employment case is that people add a non-market exchange to a market one: we are far more used to manipulations by market-makers who think up wheezes to lock us into contractual relationships, and entice us with lotteries, special offers, free gifts and the like, which may be successfully deceptive, and in any case try to make it appear that an essentially market transaction is something else.

Another area of category-play is the effort made by manufacturers to place new products as positional commodities particularly suited to gift giving. So, for instance, with those automatic tea-makers incorporating an alarm clock, which could be set to fill a tea-pot with a precisely measured amount of boiling water at the desired time. They were introduced in the 1950s and 1960s and were advertised at first as an exceptional luxury for the relatively wealthy, automating the otherwise occasionally irksome routine of processing tea and distributing it in the early morning. When the machines were reasonably established (they had in the words of one commenter 'saturated' AB social groups) the manufacturers advertised the machines to CD groups as an established luxury now within grasp. The hope, in part fulfilled I believe, was that the machines could be sold as positional goods to successively poorer groups of the population, and that once they were established through gift giving, they would become household necessities. The same strategy was used for electric toothbrushes at about the same time, with the same hope that exceptional purchases for gift giving would eventually convert into routine buying from the household budget.

New goods can easily pass as positional goods, and it is interesting that manufacturers tried to sell some of them as gifts, and to identify the relationship in which they might be given – husbands and wives, for example, giving automated tea-machines. Firms which advertise humdrum commodities as ideal for gifts are attempting to persuade future customers, and they try to manipulate categories, for instance by drawing a picture with a caption: 'You owe it to your teeth to give them an electric tooth brush. They'll love you all the more for giving them an x.' The play on words, the ambiguity which insinuates giving while encouraging end-purchasers, are moderately sophisticated examples of the category campaign.

The free gift is a different case. The manufacturer of an established commodity such as breakfast cereals attempts to establish repeat sales (commitment) by including one item of a set of quite different objects in each packet, in the hope that someone will begin to collect the whole set. Cigarette cards are an interesting case because schoolchildren created a secondary series of exchanges. Some tried to collect a whole set by swapping duplicates with other children; and they also invented gambling games, one on the lines of marbles, another relying on the serial numbers of the cards. That was a single-good economy, with at least two kinds of exchange. The advantage to the cigarette manufacturers was assumed to be that children's interest in the cards would influence the smoker's choice of brand – though the systems of secondary exchange may in fact have reduced that pressure on parents and others. The same assumption underlies the provision of plastic toys, tokens ('Collect ten tokens and send off for your free space crawler') and trinkets which are packaged with breakfast cereals, or handed out with petrol.

A free gift is free because it is unsolicited, freely given. It is not free because it is costless, and it is only partly unencumbered with obligation. When I give you a present, you are obliged. When manufacturers give you a water glass or a spaceman token they hope you will be obliged, by other people or by your desire to complete a set of glasses, to buy more of their brand of whatever it may be.

This too is a manipulation of categories: an attempt, presumably successful often enough to make it worthwhile, to pass a costed item as a gift; and, in the case of cigarette cards at least, to exploit a passionate economy of secondary exchanges in order to secure a market advantage. While electric toothbrushes are supported by persuasion, the free gift, which is not costless and is intended to encumber the recipient with obligation, is an exercise of power: you have no choice but to pay for it; and you may be hooked.

Confidence tricksters are also category manipulators: they disguise theft as something else, usually a market deal on favourable terms: marks are usually persuaded by greed to buy the Eiffel Tower at a specially reduced price. But some confidence men and women run bogus charities, and I have heard an apocryphal tale from three sources which relies precisely on the victim's benevolence and charity. A couple, newly arrived in Rome (or Athens or Madrid) returned home one evening to find their car missing. They informed the police and insurance company, and went to bed. The next morning their car was outside the apartment block with a note:

> Dear neighbour: forgive me for borrowing your car without permission, but last night my daughter was taken ill, and when the ambulance didn't arrive and her convulsions got worse, I was desperate and used your Mercedes to take her to hospital. The doctors say we saved her life.
>
> My wife and I were to have gone to the theatre tonight, but we spend all our time at the little one's bedside, and cannot use these tickets. Would you accept them as a token of our gratitude, and go in our place? When this crisis is over we hope to make your acquaintance in a more conventional way, to repeat our apologies in person, and to express our gratitude again for your involuntary help.

The couple called off the police, told their insurers and went out to the theatre that evening. When they got back, however, they found that thieves had been with a removal van and had stripped their apartment of all their possessions.

These are all cases in which people use the ambiguity and complexity of exchange in a creative and adventurous way. They can do so as Trobrianders did, to protect themselves from political ambition; they can give gifts to secure market advantage as petrol retailers do; if Akerlof is right they can add non-market exchanges to market ones to ensure dignity and respect and commitment, and thieves can lure gullible people with the promise of profit or of loss.

These manipulations are ones in which social power is more or less diffuse, and does not present as control or constraint exercised by specifiable individuals or institutions. But in many relationships people do have power to control the definitions of terms and categories, and hence of the terms of exchange.

Britons, for instance, like many other Europeans, think that marriage is a relationship of 'whole persons'. While labour power can be sold to an employer, labour in marriage is not marketable but exchanged on some other basis. Economists frequently illustrate the working of national accounts by pointing out that when a man marries his housekeeper (it seems to be a very old joke) gross national product declines because even though the same work is done it is not defined as employment. People condemn payments to surrogate mothers because that service engages functions which cannot be notionally detached and transacted, but are an essential part of the integrity of a person; marriage and the market are incompatible because we think that marriage requires trust and commitment which are created by other means than market exchanges.

But that is an ideal expectation, and the realities of Britons' marriages are much more varied. In particular it is instructive to consider the ways in which people distribute income within their households; that is to say, how spouses transform money (wages, welfare payments, dividends) which they get by various means outside the home, into the common resource of a connubium. Although government agencies consider that household income is distributed evenly (so that the level of wealth or poverty is undifferentiated within the home), Jan Pahl has been able to identify three ways, broadly defined, in which earners allocate funds. When money is very short, it seems that husbands may give all their income to their wives, and receive spending money; this 'whole wage system' is also attested as common practice in some anciently poor areas among agricultural labourers. The wife manages the domestic economy, but Pahl thinks that any appearance of domestic control by women is probably an illusion: the husband abdicates in a chronic crisis ('I don't mind what she does with the money provided there's food on the table and the clothes are neat and tidy and . . .'); in conditions of acute scarcity, management is an additional burden rather than a source of power. In the allowance system, the husband gives a weekly sum to his wife which is not related particularly to his income but to some locally accepted idea of what is appropriate. This is sometimes called the wife's wage, and it can be convenient to a husband because extra income – from overtime, from increases in pay – can be concealed from his wife, and sometimes is: the wage bears no necessary relation to the resources available. In pooling systems, commonest where both spouses earn, 'we keep the purse in the drawer and take money out when it is needed'. Even here, however, the expenditures are not always equally shared: wives' earnings are earmarked for household necessities, and for homemaking, while men have their own necessary expenditures on activities outside the home. Many couples seem to combine more than one method, and to use more than one method during their marriage.

Pahl collected her data from a relatively small sample, in special circumstances; she supplements it with material from other studies and shows that the transformation from market to connubium is made in a variety of ways, from pooling to paying a wage, and recreating a 'market' within the household. Her study has obvious implications for social policy: it is wrong to assume that income is distributed equally within a household. So far as category control is concerned, it is clear that what people choose is affected not only by social class, geography, ethnicity, but by stage in the life cycle and by who earns the money or is entitled to welfare benefit.

Another example of power to define categories is the phenomenon of patron–client relationships, studied particularly by anthropologists of the Mediterranean and of South-East Asia. In general terms it is an elementary form of political life, one of the three logical possibilities open to weak persons confronted with more powerful ones: they can run away; they can combine to resist; they can submit and make the best of it. In essence, patron–clientage is a dynamic and personal relationship in which clients acknowledge the dominance of a patron, and then try to restrain him with social ties. Some are successful to a limited extent.

So in southern Europe poor labourers attached themselves if they could to landowners and merchants and became dependants; they then tried to clothe their weakness with friendship, gift exchange and godparenthood. The basic contract of employment, sharecropping or tenancy was overlain with constraining social and religious convention. Silverman, in a study which has general implications, notes that in Colleverde in central Italy the amount of goods and services which flowed from patrons to clients was much less than people said it was. The patrons would indeed provide services over and above the terms of the share-cropping contracts: they would 'lend money or guarantee loans, find work for family members not needed on the farm, obtain medical services', but the rhetoric of patronage exaggerated the actual downward movement of real goods and services. In part this was a tactic by clients: a reputation for *noblesse* might oblige a patron to act effectively and generously. In part it was a failure of patrons to deliver: they made promises and insinuated favours which they had no intention of granting; the promise was none the less obliging. Campbell, contrasting shepherds and peasants in Greece, notes that wholesale agricultural merchants were in a much stronger position vis-à-vis would-be client peasants than cheese merchants were vis-à-vis sheepherders: the agricultural merchants cheated peasants, and had far fewer ties with them, than the cheese merchants did.

Patrons offer protection in conditions where people are persuaded that they need it: Silverman indeed suggests that in Colleverde patrons went to some lengths to create the conditions in which their social inferiors would perceive that protection was necessary, and although they did not use violence, other protectors do. The distinction between those who protect citizens' life and property from disorder and war, and those who create the threats against which they then offer protection, is clearly crucial to all justifications of the Leviathan. Charles Tilly has argued forcefully that in practice it has often been difficult to distinguish protection rackets, mafias and the like, from states which collect taxes and provide state's men with a living in exchange for defence and internal order. It may well be that as many people lose lives and property in a state as in a camorra. Clearly, in each case the protectors constrain the protected persons; and Tilly is provoking when he suggests that the distinction state's men often make between extortion and the social contract is also a manifestation of social power. Social power is also at play among the categories of the economy of love and fear – Boulding's striking characterization of welfare economics – as it is in patronage and British marriages.

Exchanges involve categories, classifications of intended results, commodities and relationships. These are complicated, imprecise and incomplete, and allow relatives, employers, companies, spouses, patrons, mafiosi and state's men scope for manoeuvre and manipulation. That is an important form of social creativity, an exercise in ingenuity which is enthralling and impressive even while it may offend our sense of justice and fair play. The power to manipulate categories is unevenly distributed in populations.

Markets and
metaphors

So far marketists have had their own field of play, and I have tacitly allowed their claim that there are markets, and that these are indeed susceptible to market analysis. But it is now time to consider the ethnography of markets. For although I have argued that those exchanges which are not obviously and on the surface based on market exchange are not underlain by market principles at some deeper level either; and although I also found it difficult to follow Sahlins, and incidentally Godelier, in allowing that some economies are 'market-dominated', it is none the less true that many peoples have places of exchange which you can quite reasonably call markets and marketplaces. The question arises whether these are governed by a market principle of the kind deployed by neo-classical economists.

The starting place might well be the markets of the Tiv, a Nigerian people studied by Paul and Laura Bohannan in the years 1949–53. They give an account of the weekly Ticha market which served a number of Tiv settlements, over a period of some months in 1949–50. About 2,000 people attended the market, and most people (four-fifths of the women and half the men) brought something to sell. The most important item was locally produced rice, which was sold mainly to middlemen: in 1950, about 11 tons a day in season. That was serious business. The market was also attended by butchers, men who toured the local markets with their animals, slaughtering a few each morning, and selling the meat. And Tiv people took yams, cassava, salt, cotton in varying quantities. They met each other, and also Hausa traders and craftsmen tailors, for example, and Ibo middlemen.

Tiv thought it mildly improper for women to go to market without some goods to trade: markets were centres of all sorts of different activity, and it was possible that if a woman did not go for trade, she might be going to plot with her kinsmen, or to conduct a liaison or whatever. So many women took small quantities of goods, and set them out on the ground for sale. The Bohannans counted the goods of three women:

A   2 calabashes of groundnuts; 9 sweet potatoes; ¼ beer bottle of red palm oil.

B   5 small piles of sweet potato; 1 lb of rice; gourd seeds; sauce; a small piece of meat; 3 pennies; 3 ginger roots; 3 yams; 2 empty bottles.

C   2*d.*-worth of okra in ½*d.* piles; peppers; half a calabash of millet; a pot of oil; 2 plantains; a spool of hand-spun cotton thread.

Most of the sellers in the market had goods of this kind and quantity: they were small part-time traders who went to Ticha because it could be useful and was usually fun. It was not merely a place to buy and sell but, just as importantly, to dance, celebrate, meet friends, do politics, fix assignations and drink beer. The sociability of the market was one reason so many people attended it, dealing in minute quantities of goods. And Tiv had more than one market which they went to. People would go to Ticha market on its day, to Iyon market on its day, and so on. The Tiv week had only five days, and the days were named after the market held on that day: so Ticha was a place, a market, and (for the people who went there) the name of a day of the week. Other Tiv who attended a different market on that day called the day by a different name.

The Bohannans make it quite clear that this was in economic terms a system of free markets: prices for instance fluctuated by season and from year to year; and there was no attempt by political authorities to fix prices or to interfere with the terms of trade. In fact that would have been difficult since the Tiv did not buy by weight or by capacity, and the only people who measured quantities in Tiv markets were the Bohannans themselves. The markets were also the means of substantial movements of goods: rice from Ticha moved to another bigger market a few days away, and from there, through the work of several middlemen in sequence, passed into the regional and national economy, presumably ending up in the stalls and shops of Lagos and Ibadan. People also got things at Ticha and other local markets which they did not produce, as well as exchanging things which were the normal and usual Tiv things which every household possessed. In that sense, Ticha market was a market.

However, Ticha had several interesting features, leading to the conclusion that it was not a spontaneous or natural manifestation of some economistic hidden hand, but was a social creation, made and sustained for political and religious as well as economic motives. You have to know that Tiv organized themselves in lineages, each with elders and a territory; and that lineages were hostile – at least there was no guarantee of a peaceful welcome for strangers. And the Bohannans did witness a 'market war' which involved nearly a thousand warriors and some blood, arising out of a market quarrel. Peace, the peace of the market, was an essential element in an economic system which undoubtedly had free prices and undoubtedly caused or permitted the movement of goods from producers to consumers.

In so far as Tiv succeeded in making a peace, they did it with political strength and religious sanction. Ticha market, for instance, was started up by a teacher who wanted a place near at hand where his school could buy and sell produce. It was 'his' market, he owned it, and after a while he tried to levy tribute from buyers and sellers in return for the peace which he guaranteed. He came a cropper: people refused to pay; he had no real political standing, and the market was moved to another lineage territory where there were really powerful elders who could to the job properly. They had an *akombo*, a spiritually powerful object which lent its authority to that of the elders who instructed it to punish anyone who caused trouble in the market, and who made a sacrifice to seal the orders. These were therefore consecrated markets, 'real markets' Tiv called them, contrasting them with places or days like Ticha which were really just beer-drinks.

Making the peace of the market was therefore both political and religious, and it was an important step in a man's political career when he was strong enough to establish his ownership of a market: he got revenues; his name increased. People brought not only goods to his market for sale, but also their political and legal disputes: he would sit in judgement, arbitrate and hope to increase his standing and respect. Anthropologists and some others point often enough to the non-economic reasons people go to market, to the elements

of St Giles' Fair, to funfair aspects as well as the commercial ones.
And no doubt this is true, and is an important part of our experience
of markets. But the essential point is that Tiv markets were not
natural emanations of profit-motivated rationality, but were the
creations of politically ambitious men, using political and religious
sanctions to create the peace of the market and to enhance their
own political position. The *akombo*-guaranteed market was a
manifestation not of commodity-fetishism but of the hunger for
political power and renown.

This pattern, the Tiv political model of market exchange, seems
to be fairly widespread. It fits with Pirenne's account of early
mediaeval Europe, and also with other contemporary cases: the
market system of Morocco, the economy of Malay fisherman.
These were all dependent market systems, created under political
and spiritual protection and ambition.

Let me now present a rather different example of commercially
sophisticated traders and shopkeepers in Libya in the 1970s. The
18,000 or so Zuwaya lived in eastern Libya, and about a third of
them controlled Kufra, which is an archipelago of thirteen oases in
the central Sahara, 1,000 kilometres from Benghazi on the Mediterranean coast, and about 1,500 kilometres from Khartoum in Sudan.
Kufra has abundant water and was an inescapable stop for travellers
on the long journey between Mediterranean and African civiliz-
ations. Zuwaya thought of themselves as traders, even though
relatively few of them worked at it full-time. They certainly
dominated traffic through the Sahara in the past: many of the
merchants were Zuwaya, and Zuwaya protected and guided those
who were from other tribes: it was a protection racket, since
Zuwaya themselves were the chief danger a non-Zuwayi merchant
might encounter.

In the 1970s about two hundred Zuwaya men in Kufra got their
living principally from trade, and many more got a subsidiary
income from shopkeeping. The volume of trade was quite substantial: between six and eight 20-ton Mercedes trucks a day travelled to
Kufra, and in season about half carried on south to Chad or Sudan.
Many of the small shopkeepers of the oases had their own transport:
Toyota pick-ups were the favoured vehicle, carrying a hun-
dredweight or two of shoes or fresh vegetables or soap. Not all loads
are equally heavy; cigarettes, for instance, are light, but relatively
bulky. You could make a very rough guess, of perhaps 100 tons of

goods arriving each week in Kufra, and rather less than half that amount continuing southwards (allowing for political restrictions on trade). The goods carried included all that was needed for a wealthy population living in a non-productive area. Most fruit and vegetables, quite a lot of meat were produced in the oases, but all other food (pasta, rice, tea, sugar, flour, cheese, tinned milk, fish, tomatoes, beans), all clothing, shoes, household equipment, insecticides, furniture were imported and carried south to Kufra. With the provision of twenty-four-hour electricity in the oases, people had begun to acquire refrigerators, air-conditioning and freezers; with the expansion of popular democracy and local control of government there had been a huge demand for office equipment – desks, chairs, filing cabinets and typewriters. And with the expansion of salary-based incomes, people began to build themselves houses of a substantial sort, requiring bricks, cement, timber, paint. And with the expansion of trade, it was important to have local supplies of fuel and spare parts for motors. All that arrived in Kufra. Zuwaya traders who continued southward usually carried cloth, subsidized foodstuffs and some household goods such as radios and electric fans, as well as occasional bargain goods and special deals for which they hoped to find a market.

Zuwaya were substantially engaged in internal commerce and exploited differences in international market prices to make what were in effect substantial incomes. They valued trade very highly: it was what they said they had always done, and it was the ideal activity of the ideal 'free Zuwayi' – a man who was beholden to no one, was not employed by another nor a servant of the state. Nevertheless, their trade had characteristics which were not those which the neo-classical model predicts.

Zuwaya tended to trade with kinsmen: the Italian conquest of Kufra in 1932 had created a substantial Zuwaya diaspora in Chad and Sudan, where there were a number of more recent refugees as well. Some men maintained two households, with a family in Libya and in sub-Saharan Africa: they trucked goods between the arms of their family firm. Within Libya traders got contracts to supply cousins or brothers who were shopkeepers or builders. Zuwaya success and confidence was built on trust in friends, kin and spouses rather than on trust in the workings of a market. Zuwaya were more confident in kin, you might say, than they were in the impartiality of economic forces; and that is how they made their money.

The evidence about Zuwaya accounting procedures tends to the same conclusion. Very few Zuwaya kept account books: in response to direct questions on the subject, the two richest men claimed to do so, and said that they kept track of their ramified enterprises with the aid of specialist accountants (of whom Libya possessed very few at that time). Two small shopkeepers showed me account books in which they kept notes of loans they had made to their friends, or credit they had granted to their customers – the distinction was vague, and the books were multi-purpose *aides-mémoire* rather than representations of the costs and returns of a business. 'Do you make a profit?' I would ask; and then, 'But how do you know you make one?' In every case (except for the two millionaires) people replied that they sold their goods for a bit more than they paid for them: you buy Korean tinned pilchards at 40 Libyan dinars a gross, and you sell at (say) 0.35LD a tin: you get 50LD in return for an outlay of 40LD, and that is a profit of 10LD. Well; it may be or it may not: most British shopkeepers for instance include more in their accounts than the cost of stock; and the notion of a rate of return over a period of time seems to be an important ingredient of capitalist calculation. Zuwaya accounting standards were less comprehensive than OECD ones, and they did not seem to use the notion that shelf-space is a valuable commodity, or that turnover is a measure of efficiency. They certainly used money to purchase commodities to sell for money; but it is not at all clear that they calculated their enterprise. They varied their prices, ate their stock, loaned their spare cash to friends for no return.

The point is that no one really knew if they were making a profit, unless they had money to spend (on more stock, on ceremonial exchange and alms-giving). What relation that money in the pocket might have to outlay, to the time taken to achieve the return, was not available knowledge: in my understanding of capitalist markets, however, those are the conventional measures of profitability of enterprise.

Another aspect of Zuwaya trade concerns risk. I think it fair to say that every trader and trucker I met was against risk, and would have been happiest to know that he had succeeded in eliminating it altogether from his enterprise. The men who considered themselves more successful, and who were generally agreed to be so, had gone some way to ensure that they did not lose money in any intrepid commercial adventure. Zuwaya associated risk with struggle, with uncertainty, and a strong man and one who could be trusted was a man who was sure, reliable, and (for instance) not likely to betray you because he was forced by circumstances to retrench or to weigh his priorities against you. Risk-taking brought the trader into a cloud of uncertainty, and that could affect his associates as well, if things turned out badly.

What I have done so far is to contrast Tiv marketers and Zuwaya entrepreneurs with an image of capitalists which is derived from market activity, mainly in Europe. In those terms, Zuwaya appear exotic, and Tiv markets decidedly imperfect. But it is clear that when you contrast them with the actions and institutions of actual capitalists (as opposed to theoretical or stereotypical ones), they do not appear so aberrant. Stock markets, commodity markets in London or New York or Chicago, local labour markets in Britain, are also associations of people, more or less formally organized and bounded, and (often) with an equal amount of face-to-face interaction and acquaintance. And it is by no means clear that a Morgan, a Carnegie, or a Nuffield would give up the opportunity to maintain a commercial advantage, even a monopoly, on the theoretical ground that the greater perfection of the market required him to do so: competition is as unwelcome to a classical entrepreneur as it was to a Zuwayi trader, and it is even more difficult to see modern corporations embracing risk for its own thrill: ICI and Siemens do not cherish adrenalin. Modern companies, at any rate in OECD countries, do produce accounts, and have got more detailed ways of identifying and forecasting profits. But it is not altogether clear that these are an objective technology of capitalist accumulation. On the one hand, some corporations go bust through their own ignorance of their internal affairs. On the other, the items which go into OECD accounts as costs and claims and capital are social categories, fluid and negotiable. Indeed many of the detailed items of accounting are related more to the requirements of taxing authorities than they are to the scientific conduct of a business.

In that regard the important fact about the Libyan state in the 1970s was that the government got its revenues from petroleum companies, and not from taxing its citizens. The Libyan socialist regime was hostile to private merchants and tried to restrict their activities in various ways, but it had no apparatus to tax them out of existence. The government did not require merchants to keep accounts, and the money-in-the-pocket test was satisfactory to all parties: merchants could believe that they were successful, and the government could argue that Libyan socialism was cankered by capitalist traders. In an OECD state the government has to tax its own citizens and the priorities are rather different. It is essential, for instance, that the citizens are productive – that they make wealth that can then be taxed, for only then can the state afford to provide them with protection and to reward the state's men for their dedication to public service. In this case it makes sense among other things to generate an expectation of rising living standards, and to establish a regulated market which approximates in some respects to the conditions of perfect competition: monopolist or corporatist citizens become too powerful vis-à-vis the government, and it is more fruitful from the revenue collector's point of view to have a large number of producers, in conditions of uncertainty, striving to produce taxable wealth. Only if the market is structured to preserve risk can government be sure that no one will succeed in eliminating competition to achieve the kind of certainty that Zuwaya traders quite reasonably regarded as the most desirable conditions of business. Only if government intervenes to prohibit insider manipulation can state's men be sure that sufficient citizens will trust the market to be impartial between them, and so enter the game of wealth creation, and so generate revenues. Accounting standards (to return to an earlier point) are one means of ensuring competition, as well as a conventional measure of the taxable profitability of market-players.

Of course, there are other differences between markets than the extent and intent of government regulation: the scale of operations varies, the kinds of goods which are traded are also important, as are the kinds of social relations among traders; and the difference between trading tribesmen and the bureaucracy of OECD corporations is also significant, although often exaggerated. But it is the case that conditions approaching perfect competition have only been achieved – as many economists point out – where governments intervene to maintain them; and this is a contradiction in terms of the nineteenth-century theories of economic competition. When that government action fails or is missing, the conditions of trade tend towards those desired by Zuwaya. The free enterprise economy relied on government to create the conditions in which it could work. An autonomous or nearly autonomous economic sphere in which exchanges are made according to principles which are closest to those of the market has to be created and maintained by political powers which get kudos and revenue from their ownership of the market and from guaranteeing it.

My conclusion is that 'the market principle' is not and never has been an autonomous reality. When exchanges are really free from control people do their best to create monopolies, to do insider trading, to eliminate risk and to exclude outsiders who might bring in competition and something approximating supply and demand. That is scarcely the market principle, but rather what market operators would really like: an easy life, with as little competition as possible, if you please. A secondary and incidental conclusion is that the rhetorical contrast made by some politicians and theoreticians in Britain and the USA, between the state and the market, assumes antagonism where there is in fact mutual dependence: the market, the Blue Economy produces revenue.

To end this chapter I want to consider one other group of people who have taken the marketistic model of exchange for real. I refer to the bundle of related theories which originated with von Mises's Praxeology in the 1940s and came to flourish as exchange theory in the 1950s and 1960s. The sociologists and anthropologists concerned took the view that the model could explain all social life (Homans), or the most important elements of it (Blau, Barth), or that it explained some activities really, and others 'as if' (Bailey). Social life, or bits of it, consisted of a series of exchanges of goods, glances, loyalty, kisses and caresses; and it could be analysed and explained with the aid of a model of rational profit motivation.

The work was quite interesting: Homans and Blau produced minute accounts of interaction in small groups. Blau further maintained that people who exchanged always had different amounts of power, and he attempted to show how those differences were perpetuated by exchange to become institutionalized into social structures: his was a model which he claimed generated social order. Barth used exchange theory mostly to explain social change: with a given social organization, people pursue their profits in social and economic exchange, and that leads them to innovate: he was fascinated by the power of entrepreneurs to create new combinations of things, and used this metaphor to model social change. Bailey also took social structure to be a relatively uninteresting given, and market-metaphorized the manoeuvres and tricks of leaders and followers to produce witty, sardonic and deeply offensive accounts of social tactics. Blau was also one of the first to use game theory to analyse the balance sheets which must underlie the profit and loss accounts of rational social exchange. This is now much more highly developed, and is used by philosophers and economists with an interest in social matters, to create models to derive altruism, trust, self-sacrifice within a general context of formal rationality. It is very elegant work, but often seems remote from the concerns of sociologists and anthropologists who are interested in long-term historical tendencies, say, or in the painful realities of income distribution within households.

I want to make two general points about the exchange theories of the 1950s and 1960s. The first is that they are not about exchange, as say number theory is about numbers. I do not think that any of the practitioners made any advances in the theory of exchange. They were much more concerned to show that everything in social life, or its more important bits, were exchange or were like exchange. In this respect exchange theories were like phlogiston theory: they were extended metaphors, as is often the case with theories which are named by their *explanans* rather than by their *explanandum*. The second point is the slightly embarrassing observation that even the anthropologists who explored the possibilities of an exchange metaphor did not consider the range of ethnographic evidence about the variety of kinds of exchange and economic motive. They were sold on marketistic rationality, and their work is therefore open to all the arguments that are advanced against the axioms, practices and conclusions of those unrealistic modellers.

Symbols and Cooked Breakfasts

I take the liberty to send you two brace of grouse, curious, because killed by a Scotch metaphysician; in other and better language they are mere ideas, shot by other ideas, out of a pure intellectual notion called a gun.

Sydney Smith to Lady Holland, 1808

Your breakfast is a symbol: you eat scrambled eggs with smoked salmon, and it means something different from eating bacon and eggs and sausages and fried bread. It has consequences and antecedents since people judge you in part by your consumption, and suggest that you are elegantly refined or gross and traditional; meanings generate other meanings, and dry toast is different from black pudding. But in addition people say that the kind of breakfast you eat affects your health and life expectancy, and that if enough people eat black pudding, black pudding makers can feed their families. Your life expectancy and the survival of an industry are not pure intellectual notions; and it is not a mere idea that people die in famines, having neither breakfast nor lunch nor dinner. On the one hand, people tend to think of symbols as somehow less real than death and happiness: they stand for things, and are not the things themselves. On the other, people certainly invest most of their actions with meaning, and their actions have consequences, so that when the meanings change, and say black pudding becomes unfashionable, the economy changes.

This final but inconclusive chapter is an exploration of the fact that people load their exchanges with meaning, and that exchanges are symbols: they have consequences not only for life itself, but for the meaning of life as well. So the question arises, to what extent can you explain differences among economies by the meanings which people attach to their actions? One of the problems in that inquiry is that studies of symbols are apparently less precise and fixed than the realities of birth, death, disease, happiness and nourishment. You can tell fairly easily whether a person is alive or dead; it is more difficult to know what someone means when they offer you bread or a stone.

That is partly because of the character of symbols: it is generally agreed at any rate among anthropologists that the meaning of a symbol cannot be translated into a word, and that a string or bundle of symbols does not have another form as a sentence: they evoke rather than denote, and for this reason they can mean different things to different people, or to the same person on different occasions. A further problem is that people can be led to believe that they understand symbols intuitively: they are non-verbal communication and, just as I think I can understand Russian music without speaking Russian or knowing very much about Russian culture, so I may think I understand symbols used in Tierra del Fuego or the Sepik River, by my natural endowment of sensitive responsiveness and universal intuition; I could be mistaken, but it is rather more difficult to show me that I am than it is to show me that I have misunderstood the gross meaning of a sentence. So although symbols evoke other things, and although people can intend them to mean something very precise (red roses, eternity rings, a meal to invite people to) they can be even more easily misunderstood than words.

Some anthropologists used to think that symbols formed a flexible system of items which had regular connections, a sort of grammar, among them. But, as Sperber has pointed out, whatever connections they may have do not allow the kinds of transformation which are enabled by a grammar (for example, from singular to plural, from past to present, negative to interrogative to conditional to positive). The connections are quite unlike a grammar, and anthropologists and literary critics seem now to think of them as like figures of speech: analogy, metaphor, metonymy, synecdoche (but oxymoron, like some others, is silently absent from the range).

These two difficulties (that symbols are not like words, and that the connections among them are not like a grammar) are the consequence of the character of symbols. They make it very difficult to analyse the symbols people use, even though we know that some of the meaning of people's lives is gained and expressed through symbols, and that many or most of their actions, including exchanges, have an intrinsic symbolic component. Additional difficulties arise from the way scholars have studied symbols. In particular, and most important for present purposes, anthropologists are uncertain what entities there may be in a mental world: symbols, obviously; but do ideas, emotions, jokes, languages count as symbols, and have similar constructive force in those worlds? I think the answer is unclear, for it is difficult to discern from the varying practice of the experts, what they consider their field to consist of, or what relation there is among the different kinds of thing which may be found in it.

Students of symbols have underemphasized the fact that symbols are both conventionally public and also privately expressive. Lady Harriet humiliated Mrs Carlyle by giving her a cook's gift: that was a gesture that everyone could understand, even if perhaps some bystanders thought it quite inappropriate. But in addition to that the gift had meanings which were more or less private to Mrs Carlyle: it was one of a series of minor humiliations, it insinuated a distinction between husband and wife, all in ways which were not conventional, or even part of the general social knowledge of the Christmas party – the meanings of the gift were restricted. Indeed Lady Harriet said, with tears in her eyes, that she had not intended them. Clearly, these meanings are not a constant: some exchanges are fairly casual, and some people read more into actions than others do, are more sensitive to innuendo and hidden significance. We simply do not know whether a Trobriander, receiving a basket of yams, attached private meanings to it. Malinowski records that they assessed the value of kula armshells and necklaces very carefully, and no doubt they worked out the meaning of particular kula exchanges; Trobrianders were also fairly sharp when they bartered useful things, and I suppose that they used their faculty of assessment in other exchanges. I guess that some Trobrianders were touchier than others, that some grumbled that they should have received an axe-blade, or that the yams were disrespectfully poor quality. We know that givers of yams tried to make the best ones most visible; but we do not know whether a man might fail to do so when the gift was for a person he didn't respect, or wished to insult. My guess is that Trobrianders were and are as variably subtle in these matters as Britons are, but I don't know. And this is generally the case with anthropological studies of symbols: we have paid little attention to private or restricted meanings and have concentrated on public ones.

In addition to that kind of meaning, people play with the symbolism of exchange. For instance, when A. Strathern (then widely known for his analyses of New Guinea exchanges of pigs) became Professor of Social Anthropology at University College London, his colleagues instituted a series of exchanges with their new Bigman using china, cloth, wooden representations of pigs – a joking, inventive and complimentary welcome and an invitation to collegiality and anthropological in-groupishness. It was play-exchange, with in-group meanings, and invented to convey friendly messages about the future. Once again, we simply do not know that this kind of play-exchange, laden with private messages, is available throughout the world: you might guess that it is, but nobody really knows – although Hyde suggests that many Americans play-exchange. Playing with symbols to convey meanings may be an important creative activity everywhere, but we don't really know that it is.

A further important issue is whether some exchanges symbolize more than others do. Mauss certainly thought so, for he was committed to the view that in early societies gift exchange was a prestation totale. Potlatch, for example, involved the total social personality of the giver and receiver: what a Kwakiutl potlatcher gave was not just blankets, oil, fish, a copper, but his standing, his ritual and political self as well as his material goods. Potlatches were agonistic, because the rule of exchange was that the person who received goods had to try to return more: only one of the two exchangers could meet that obligation and hence one of them was inevitably diminished in his political, religious and economic standing. In success or failure, a potlatcher constituted himself. That line of argument has important and significant adherents today, for example in the work of M. Strathern. I think I am right to say that she argues that some New Guinea Highlanders use exchange to symbolize themselves: it is their whole being which is given. And she uses the symbolism of gifts (a broadly hewn category in her writing) to argue further that while OECD persons (with perhaps some reservations about say Japanese) use the categories man, woman, individual, society as fairly fixed points of reference, it is interesting and stimulating to try to approximate to an ineffable perception that New Guinea Highlanders use them fluidly and conventionally, defining and redefining themselves in the processes of their exchange. In short, Mount Hageners and others live in a world which is created by the meanings of their exchanges: an allotropic universe whose content at any one moment is defined by the meanings of the exchanges which are then in process.

Mauss was quite clear in his mind that OECD exchanges are thinner, and that we evoke less, involve less of our total social personalities than Kwakiutl or Trobrianders do. It does seem true from introspection that my actions in a supermarket are less than a prestation totale, just as my gender and individuality are not allotropically defined by my exchanges. So Mauss's account rings true: if Mount Hageners do define their existence with their exchanges, then it must be that they give them more meaning than Britons do. However, ringing true is not a good guide to truth, but a warning bell against the danger of making assumptions: if an idea slips easily into the mind, better assume that it is likely wrong. And in fact, while it is quite common to find students of symbols saying or implying that some symbols carry more weight than others do, it is very rare to find that they use anything other than intuition to assess the more and the less. Anthropologists lack a means of measuring the quanta of social personality which are loaded on to exchanges, and cannot assess the thickness of layers of meaning. So, although it is trivial, I prefer to say provisionally that the amount of meaning which Britons load on to their exchanges is neither more nor less than Mount Hageners or Kwakiutl do: my exchanges define and maintain me in the social persona of a male Briton with roughly identifiable characteristics, and fixed in an individualistic marketing economy. It is not an ideal solution, but it is safer, when confronted with allegations of differences on a scale which has no markers, to assume that the differences do not exist. In spite of Mauss, I therefore assume that the amount of meaning carried by exchanges is a constant, is uniformly thick.

A further problem is that it is uncertain who has to understand a symbol or string or bundle of symbols for them to be included among the furniture of a world. Although we can read and write with pleasure and contentment about say Tiv symbols, it is quite clear some Tiv understand them more than others do: children generally understand less than old people, some old people are more expert than others, and so on. Anthropologists write rather little about such uneven distribution, and produce generalized accounts of 'the' symbolic 'system' of the natives of this place or that. In fact, however, some meanings are widely shared and understood, others less so. A Trobriander who started a valuable off on its path put himself at risk, and everyone who knew that he had done so understood this. Only some of the people present understood why Mrs Carlyle was so upset; but since understanding was available to them, you can allow that as a common understanding. Other symbols are restricted to groups (members of a sect, of a college or coterie) and categories (men, women, young men, young women). And some symbols are intelligible only to anthropologists, and to those who then read their books: you might wish to put those meanings into a special category. My main concern is the way British and other natives load meanings on to their actions, and I am only secondarily concerned with those hidden realities. (We do know that the texture of a native world changes when some of its inhabitants read about their deeper structures: the works of Adam Smith, Marx, Darwin, Frazer and Freud have all changed our understanding of our world. But we have little information on what happens when anthropologists bring the deep structures of symbolism to the surface. Perhaps they too are underlain by structures which had previously been too deep even for seismologists of ideas to discover.) So note that anthropologists often load specialized and private meanings on to the actions they describe; and consider that it may be sensible to regard these as of a different kind than those (variably accessible) meanings which are home-grown in their native soil. It is unfortunately true that many students of symbols have found it difficult to maintain that distinction, just as they often assume an evenly spread native understanding of local symbols.

Symbols are intrinsically difficult to analyse, since they have meanings which are indeed meanings but which are not expressed in words, and are not connected as words are. In addition, studies of symbols at present reveal: an unexplored relation between symbols and other mental tools; weakness of evidence about private symbols and play-exchanges; uncertainties whether some exchanges symbolize more than others, and an indefiniteness about who understands a symbol. In short, contemporary studies of symbols are too imprecise to sustain the position that the world is a pure intellectual notion, and that each native or set of natives inhabits their own constructed world. You can see the attraction of such a position to sensitive OECD natives: in hegemonistic and materialist states, it is comforting to assert the relativity of values and the unreality of material. But it seems premature to take a decision in principle while the new worlds are so arbitrarily approximate.

So the position is that we know that people load meanings on to their actions – that human actions are intrinsically meaning-laden. And we know that those meanings are real and variable and allusive, slippery, evocative. I want now to consider what we can say about the consequences of meaning, what part meaning should have in an explanation of differences among economies.

Money is commonly said to be a symbol of value and a means of exchange and (when it doesn't deteriorate) a store of wealth. We owe to Codere an important decomposition of the notion of money. The force of her argument is that we think of money as inevitably associated with other symbolic orders, even though that is not essentially the case. For instance, we think of money as an aspect of number: you have tenpence; you buy something; you get twopence change. You promise to pay £50 a month, and you can multiply that, and know you will pay £600 a year. Money and number are associated, and we can add, subtract, divide and multiply what we quite unselfconsciously call sums of money.

But number is not part of money; it is an independent set of symbols. We certainly know of peoples who have number, but do not have money; and we know of one economy which had money without number. That was on Rossell Island which is part of the Louisiade Archipelago to the south-east of New Guinea. Coins were large stones, which certainly symbolized value, but in an ordinal system: some were worth more than others, but there was no numerical relation between them. If you wanted to borrow money, you borrowed a particular coin, and repaid it later with one a point or two up the scale. You could not add one coin to another. Similarly, Salisbury writes of the Siane that they categorized New Guinea pennies as things of no account, silver shillings as valuables: they considered it improper to convert valuables into ordinary things, and so shillings were not convertible into pennies: you could not get change for a shilling. To a limited extent, Siane had symbols of value which were not convertible by a numerical relation.

The power of numbered money in our societies is also associated with all those other numeric orders which we use to express amounts: pints and litres, ounces, grams, feet, metres, bushels, quintals. These are ancillary systems, also dependent on number, of vast importance but not necessarily associated with money. The Tiv did not use a system of weights and measures – it was the Bohannans who weighed goods coming into Ticha market. However, once people have established the association, it is consequential: you can compare prices and standardize them; it makes it possible to regulate prices, for example; and it makes it much easier to collect taxes and exchange commodities. Without a series of weights and measures it would have been very difficult for political authorities to set prices in a Tiv market. If a pile of peppers costs ½ *d*., and the government fixes the price at ¼ *d*., the seller can divide her pile into two. The government has control only if it can say '100 grams of peppers shall cost ¼ *d*.'

The third element of the symbolic complex which we call money is writing and its surrogates: we can write cheques, for instance, and acquire goods without carrying specie in our pockets. We can also trade and deal with the goods in one place and the money in another: a sum of money is transferred from one account to another, and doesn't change hands in any material sense at all. Without writing it is really quite difficult to keep accounts of any great complexity, to calculate profit and loss or to forecast cash-flows and capital investment even though you may have weights and measures and an intricate arithmetic. The basis of industrial and commercial activities is not simply money, but money *and* number *and* amounts *and* writing.

So, Codere's work suggests that the symbolic order which we call money, and think of as a unitary system, is in fact a composite, a complex and non-essential set of relations between different sets of symbols. Moreover, it has consequences: when the Tiv began to acquire money and to use it fairly frequently, the old conventions of exchange, that some things could not be traded against each other, broke down, and that may have been a consequence of the power of money; clearly, commerce and industry function more quickly and with fewer incidental costs when buyers do not transfer specie to sellers. It is also the case that with electronic or paper transfers of money, it does not become physically scarce. In Italy, for instance, you used quite often to be given sweets or telephone tokens instead of the smaller denominations of specie, simply because there was a shortage of 5 and 10 lire coins. At an autostrada toll-booth it was amusing for a while to wait behind a Swedish or Dutch car while the attendant explained that the glacier mints were in lieu of 5 lire coins, and further, that his colleague at the next booth down the road would not accept toffee in payment. In the smaller towns and villages of southern Italy in the 1950s there were general shortages of cash after the tax-paying season; and hence, increased use of credit and payments in kind. So writing produces speedy and cheap transactions, and avoids shortages of specie and indeed creates the possibility of circulating money very quickly and using it several times over, while a more cumbersome physical money moves more slowly. The most valuable coins of Rossell Island incidentally were so heavy that they couldn't be moved at all; and that presumably had the same effect as making them electronic and insubstantial: Rossell Islanders, too, did not have to waste time moving money.

To sum up: money is a complex not a simple order of symbols, associating money, weights and measures, writing. It is my guess that all symbolic orders are of this kind: all are composites, and juxtaposed with others. And the associations of money have consequences: it seems to be more powerful the more it is associated with other sets of symbols, and money exchanges seem to displace other kinds of exchange even though Siane spheres of exchange resisted the universalizing tendencies of money at least for a while.

Money is a special case among symbols because OCED natives at any rate can mint it, control the quantities of it, count it, measure the flow of it. That allows anthropologists to be more precise about money than they can be about many other symbols which are not measurable. Some people think that because it is measurable, money is somehow less poetic than real symbols are: real symbols (they suggest) evoke vaguely and elusively, and are a nobler manifestation of human creativity than crass brass. Perhaps that is not a difference in principle, however: it does seem to be the case that in some ways money is evocative and allusive, as well as measurable – it is a mistake to regard it as simply vulgar. And again it is only some peoples, as Codere has shown, who associate their symbols of value with numbers, measures and writing: presumably for them money is decently vaguer than it is for us. It is the association which allows us to pin down highly resonant symbols of something so nebulous as value (and to diminish it in the process), and it is not, you might say, money itself which is distasteful.

Does money provide any answer to the question I started out from: what part might symbols have in an explanation of differences among economies? It helps in two ways: first, it shows symbols to be consequential; second, it suggests how consequences are brought about.

Money is consequential for economies: it affects transaction costs, allows state intervention, simplifies accounting procedures, allows people to save. These are real effects. And it is not only money which has consequences for economy. Christmas wrapping paper effectively evokes festivity and generosity and the fun and pleasure of exchange; it leads people to buy and make more goods than they would otherwise, and it integrates productive effort both by firms and by private individuals. But some symbols are more consequential than others: OECD money more than Christmas wrapping paper, for instance, and Christmas wrapping paper more than an eternity ring. Of course these are in most respects incommensurable: the right promise of eternal love can be very consequential, and the meanings are real and important. But OECD money has consequences for more people and for a greater range of their actions and relationships, than symbols of undying love which are exchanged between two happy people. The reality of the symbols in each case is not in question; but their consequentiality is very different. The Bohannans argue that OECD money is more powerful than indigenous Tiv money: this is partly a matter no doubt of the backing of the colonial state which levied its taxes in state money rather than brass rods; but the Bohannans also suggest that it was symbolically more powerful as well.

In the case of money, greater power and consequentiality derive from association: it is because symbols of value are associated with number and measures and writing that OECD money is said to be more powerful than other less associated moneys. It is the juxtaposition of these elements which makes money evocative of a range of valuables: one dancing partner or twenty oranges or a motor car. Juxtaposition seems to be a sufficient explanation of greater and lesser consequentiality, at least in this case.

Exchanges are complex categories, and the categorization

associates desired outcomes, commodities and relationships; each of the components evokes the others and suggests meaning. So, I may give you a gift for the first time, and that indicates something about the kind of relationship we have, and what I would like it to be in the future. If you then say 'Oh, but you must let me pay you for it', you too indicate your view of how we stand to each other. Urigubu not only maintained a relationship, but symbolized it, as is shown by the Omarakana harvest of 1918: by giving urigubu rather than tribute, people were able to resist the chief's claim of authority. The associations among the elements of the exchange evoke each other, and are conventionally (legally, morally, religiously) juxtaposed. Manufacturers give free gifts, in the hope of establishing brand loyalty; and, if Akerlof is right, employers and employees exchange work, effort and wages above the going market rates in order to establish commitment and fair dealing of a non-market kind. These are consequential because they have effects on all aspects of social life, as well as economy. They are not just aesthetic frills, tacked on to the real business of market-wise operations: Akerlof seeks to explain involuntary unemployment, no less.

Giving good measure, a baker's dozen, a fair day's work, have consequences for economic performance, as do the trust and friendliness, indifference to persons, benevolence to the sick, compassion to the poor, fear of the mob which we convey in our exchanges. Trobrianders' productive effort was also integrated by a series of about eighty different kinds of exchange, each with a roughly specifiable public meaning. These also have consequences for the feel of economies: the experience of working and consuming in an OECD state, in Libya or Tivland or the Trobriands is different. And meanings, symbols, are as real as death and smoked salmon.

Can the variability of meaning explain why some people have food while others starve? Famine is not a natural disaster, a mechanical product of drought, poor technology and overpopulation, but is a consequence of social organization, among other things of distribution systems. It is therefore a matter of kinds of exchange, of the means by which people move food from one person to another. You can ask why people do not have particular kinds of exchange, of the sort which might enable them to relieve or prevent famine, but it is an unsatisfactory answer to say 'they don't have the intentions and meanings which would require the symbols which would require new kinds of exchange'. It is unsatisfactory because in intellectual terms we do not understand enough about symbolism; and in practical terms it seems likely that we understand better how to manipulate institutions than symbols: at any rate in the short term, it is more sensible to regard kinds of exchange as determining, rather than the meanings which people attach to them.

Further Reading

Here are some of the main sources of the ideas and information in the text. It is not intended as a general bibliography.

Chapter 1

The main general anthropological accounts of exchange are by Mauss (1954), Malinowski (1922), Firth (1967) and Sahlins (1972b). Panoff (1970) is still interesting, and I have also found Hyde (1979) stimulating and thoughtful. The more recent collections of essays edited by Appadurai (1986) and by Parry and Bloch (1989) amount to surveys of exchange or exchange-related topics, and the introductions attempt a general review of the fields. The work of Lévi-Strauss (1968; 1969) is regarded as crucial by many people, especially because he uses an exchange model to explain the generation of human society. That is a line of argument which is carried forward in sociology through the work of Gouldner (1960), among others. Ekeh, in a notable work (1974), attempts to reconcile a Lévi-Straussian aproach with that of American sociologists concerned with exchange theory (see Chapter 5).

Many anthropologists have produced more or less complete ethnographic accounts of exchange. Those which I find particularly stimulating, and which are not cited below, include Firth (1939; 1946), Douglas (1967), Pospisil (1972), and Strathern (1971).

Sociologists of economic life are not always concerned with the range of exchanges which anthropologists take for granted. A good general introduction is by Roberts et al. (1985), which contains many references. Pahl's (1984) work on Sheppey contains ethnographic information, as do a number of works on informal economy: Harding and Jenkins (1989) provide a useful survey and bibliography.

Information on Trobriand harvests is drawn from Malinowski (1965 [1935]); on the Carlyle's Christmas in Scotland from Origo (1957) and Wilson (1927; 1929). The potlatch was first described in detail by Boas

(1921) and there have been many subsequent investigations and reworkings of the material: Codere (n.d. [1950]) and Rosman and Rubel (1971) are among the more interesting.

Polanyi (1947; 1957; Polanyi *et al.*, 1957) made important pioneering contributions to the discussion of substantive economies. Dalton (1961; 1966; 1967; 1971) developed the themes, which are further elaborated by Sahlins (1972b). Cook (1966) provides a sharp critique of 'substantivist' economics. Godelier (1972) analyses Western economics as ideology, and his attempt to create a marxist ethnographic economics of non-capitalist peoples is chiefly there. The most recent attempt to produce a relativist account of economics is by Gudeman (1986).

Blue Book is the familiar term for the annual *United Kingdom National Accounts* published by the Central Statistical Office.

Chapter 2

I am not learned in economics, and I am not competent to represent the wide range of nuance in that discipline. So I have contrasted the anthropological approach to exchange with that of some strands of neo-classical economics which I characterize as 'marketist'. The claim that such economics can account for all social activity is stated clearly and elegantly by Robbins (1932; 1968), and is represented in the text by Tullock and others writing for the Institute of Economic Affairs (1973). The line of argument which analyses exchange and choice on the worst-case hypothesis (that all people are motivated by self-interest) derives ultimately from Edgeworth and Marshall. Its contemporary manifestations are not all devoted to achieving perfect competition: Collard (1978) for instance is concerned to show that it could be rational to be altruistic – a line of argument which is also present in Boulding's (1973) earlier work on welfare economics. Hollis's (1987) work which uses game theory (which is not a theory about game) to show how it might be rational to be altruistic, has its precursors in Collard (1978) and Blau (1964) among others. I have tried to avoid tarring all economists with the marketist brush, and am in fact indebted to the work of Sen (1982) and Akerlof (1984) among other things because it has helped me to perceive the subtler weaknesses of the marketist position.

For discussions of rationality see Wilson (1970), Hollis and Lukes (1982), and Godelier (1972).

The source for buritila'ulo is Malinowski's *Coral Gardens* (1965 [1935]: 182–6). Kula is described in detail in *Argonauts* (Malinowski, 1922), and there are later studies in Leach and Leach (1983) (which includes the article referred to by Edmund Leach) and Weiner (1976).

The discussion of blood donors draws on Titmuss (1969) and on a publication by the Institute of Economic Affairs (1973); see also Davis

(1973). Interestingly, Hyde (1979) also takes this case as an example of the inaptness of marketistic analysis. Charities are discussed by Nightingale (1973), where the Aberfan example is on p. 178.

Sahlins's fundamental account of his theory of reciprocal economy can be found in 'On the sociology of primitive exchange' (1965).

Chapter 3

The discussion of classification derives ultimately from the now superseded Durkheim and Mauss (1963 [1903]). For a general review of the state of the art in the mid-1970s see Ellen (1979). Functional categories are expounded in Wierzbicka (1984); pairing in Lancy and Strathern (1981). Lévi-Strauss's binary oppositions are diffused in his works, but marked in his *Savage Mind* (1967) and in *The Raw and the Cooked* (1969b). For a general account of his system, see also Leach (1970 [1984]). The notion that couples are subversive of the state (and can be favoured by state's men who wish to reduce the impact of the state and other corporations on citizens' lives) is proposed by Mount (1983). The legal classification of dogs, horses and cows is discussed by Sawyer (1965).

Chapter 4

See Sahlins (1972a) for the discussion of trading reciprocalists; and Davis (1972) for the information on gifts in the UK.

Chapter 5

Douglas (1966) is widely credited with the modern elaboration of anomaly theory, casting anomalies as essentially worrying. The description of the tribute-urigubu of 1918 in Omarakana is in Malinowski (1965 [1935]: 189-6, 210–17, 392–7). Herzfeld's account of disemia is chiefly in his *Anthropology through the Looking-Glass* (1987); and Lienhardt (1982) discusses parallax. The chief source for speculation about the importance of ambiguity and uncertainty in social order is Gellner (1970).

As indicated, Akerlof (1984) is my source for discussion of involuntary unemployment; Pahl (1983) for information on money and power within British households. The two sources for the discussion of Mediterranean patronage are Silverman (1977) and Campbell (1968). My representation of Tilly is based on Tilly (1985).

Chapter 6

For the Tiv markets see Bohannan and Bohannan (1968: esp. 146–94). Paul Bohannan (1959) has an argument about the differential power of different kinds of money. The account of the Zuwaya is drawn from Davis (1987), and from a paper to appear in Dilley (forthcoming).

The sources which I use to characterize exchange theory are: von Mises (1949); Homans (1951; 1958); Blau (1964); Barth (1966); and Bailey (1969).

Chapter 7

The more interesting analyses of the symbolism of exchange are by Schieffelin (1980), Schwimmer (1979) and (most recent and most elaborate) Strathern (1988). The illuminating early work of Sperber (1975) has been criticized and elaborated by Strecker (1988), which contains a very clear and valuable account of recent symbology.

I have used Codere (1968) and Salisbury (1962) in my discussion of money, as well as the work of the Bohannans. Rossell Island money is discussed by Baric (1964) and Armstrong (1924). My understanding of famine is from Drèze and Sen (1990).

References

Akerlof, George, A. (1984). Labor contracts as partial gift-exchange. In George A. Akerlof, *An Economic Theorist's Book of Tales. Essays that Entertain the Consequences of New Assumptions in Economic Theory*. Cambridge: Cambridge University Press, 145–71.

Appadurai, Arjun (ed.) (1986). *The Social Life of Things: Commodities in Cultural Perspective*. Cambridge: Cambridge University Press.

Armstrong, W. E. (1924). Rossell Island money: a unique monetary system. *Economic Journal*, 34, 423–9.

Bailey, Frederick G. (1969). *Stratagems and Spoils. A Social Anthropology of Politics*. Oxford: Blackwell.

Baric, Lorraine (1964). Some aspects of credit, saving and investment in a 'non-monetary' economy (Rossell Island). In Raymond Firth and Basil Yamey (eds) *Capital, Saving and Credit in Peasant Societies. Studies from Asia, Oceania, the Caribbean and Middle America*. London: George Allen & Unwin, 35–52.

Barth, Frederick (1966). *Models of Social Organisation*. Occasional papers of the RAI, 23. London: Royal Anthropological Institute.

Blau, Peter Michael (1963). *The Dynamics of Bureaucracy*. Chicago: Chicago University Press.

Blau, Peter Michael (1964). *Exchange and Power in Social Life*. NY: Wiley.

Boas, Franz (1921). *Ethnology of the Kawakiutl, Based on Data Collected by George Hunt*. Report 35. Washington, DC: Smithsonian Institute, Bureau of Ethnology.

Bohannan, Paul (1959). The impact of money on an African subsistence economy. *Journal of Economic History*, 19, 491–503.

Bohannan, Paul and Laura Bohannan (1968). *Tiv Economy*. London: Longmans, Green & Co.

Boulding, Kenneth Ewart (1973). *The Economy of Love and Fear: A Preface to Grants Economics*. Belmont, CA: Wadsworth.

Campbell, John K. (1968). Two case studies of marketing and patronage in

Greece. In J.-G. Peristiany (ed.) *Contributions to Mediterranean Sociology*. The Hague: Mouton, 143–54.

Codere, Helen (n.d. [1950]). *Fighting with Property. A Study in Kwakiutl Potlatching and Warfare*. Monographs of the American Ethnological Society XVIII. New York: American Ethnological Society.

Codere, Helen (1968). Money exchange systems and a theory of money. *Man*, 3, 557–78.

Collard, David (1978). *Altruism and Economy. A Study in Non-Selfish Economics*. Oxford: Martin Robertson.

Cook, S. (1966). The obsolete 'anti-market' mentality. A critique of the substantive approach to economic anthropology. *American Anthropologist*, 68, 323–45.

Dalton, George W. (1961). Economic theory and primitive society. *American Anthropologist*, 63, 1–25.

Dalton, George W. (1966). A note of clarification on economic surplus. *American Anthropologist*, 62, 483–90.

Dalton, George W. (1967). *Tribal and Peasant Economies*. New York: Natural History Press.

Dalton, George W. (1971). *Economic Development and Social Change. The Modernisation of Village Communities*. Garden City, NY: Natural History Press for American Museum of Natural History.

Davis, John (1972). Gifts and the UK economy. *Man*, 7, 408–29.

Davis, John (1973). The particular theory of exchange. *European Journal of Sociology*, 16, 151–68.

Davis, John (1987). *Libyan Politics: Tribe and Revolution. The Zuwaya and their Government*. London: I. B. Tauris.

Douglas, Mary (1966). *Purity and Danger*. London: Routledge & Kegan Paul.

Douglas, Mary (1967). Primitive rationing: a study in controlled exchange. In Raymond Firth (ed.) *Themes in Economic Anthropology*. London: Tavistock Publications, 119–45.

Drèze, Jean and Amartya Sen (1990). *The Political Economy of Hunger*. Oxford: Clarendon Press.

Durkheim, Émile and Marcel Mauss (1963 [1903]). *Primitive Classification*, translated by Rodney Needham. London: Cohen and West.

Edgeworth, Francis Y. (1881). *Mathematical Physics. An Essay on the Application of Mathematics to the Moral Sciences*. London.

Ekeh, Peter (1974). *Social Exchange Theory. The Two Traditions*. London: Heinemann.

Ellen, Roy F. (1979). Introductory essay. In R. F. Ellen and D. Reason (eds) *Classifications in their Social Context*. London: Academic Press, 1–32.

Firth, Raymond (1939). *Primitive Polynesian Economy*. London: Routledge & Kegan Paul.

Firth, Raymond (1946). *Malay Fisherman: Their Peasant Economy*. London: Kegan Paul/Trench, Trubner & Co.

Firth, Raymond (1967). A general comment. In Raymond Firth (ed.) *Themes in Economic Anthropology*. London: Tavistock Publications, 1–26.

Friedman, Milton (1953). *Essays in Positive Economics*. Chicago: Chicago University Press.

Gellner, Ernest A. (1970). Concepts and society. In B. R. Wilson (ed.) *Rationality*. Oxford: Blackwell, 18–49.

Godelier, Maurice (1972). *Rationality and Irrationality in Economics*. London: New Left Books.

Gouldner, Alvin W. (1960). The norm of reciprocity. A preliminary statement. *American Sociological Review*, 25, 1961–78.

Gudeman, Stephen (1986). *Economics as Culture. Models and Metaphors of Livelihood*. London: Routledge & Kegan Paul.

Harding, Philip and Richard Jenkins (1989). *The Myth of the Hidden Economy. Towards a New Understanding of Informal Economic Activity*. Milton Keynes: Open University Press.

Herzfeld, Michael (1987). *Anthropology through the Looking-Glass. Critical Ethnography in the Margins of Europe*. Cambridge: Cambridge University Press.

Hollis, Martin (1987). *The Cunning of Reason*. Cambridge: Cambridge University Press.

Hollis, Martin and Steven Lukes (1982). *Rationality and Relativism*. Oxford: Blackwell.

Homans, George Caspar (1951). *The Human Group*. London: Routledge & Kegan Paul.

Homans, George Caspar (1958). Social behavior as exchange. *American Journal of Sociology*, 63, 597–606.

Hyde, Lewis (1979). *The Gift. Imagination and the Erotic Life of Property*. New York: Vintage Books.

Institute of Economic Affairs (1973). *The Economics of Charity. Essays on the Comparative Economics and Ethics of Giving and Selling, with Applications to Blood*. Vol. 12, Readings. London: IEA.

Lancy, David F. and Andrew J. Strathern (1981). Making twos: pairing as an alternative to the taxonomic mode of representation. *American Anthropologist*, 83, 773–95.

Leach, Edmund R. (1984). *Lévi-Strauss*. London: Collins.

Leach, Jerry W. and Edmund R. Leach (eds) (1983). *The Kula. New Perspectives on Massim Exchange*. Cambridge: Cambridge University Press.

Lévi-Strauss, Claude (1967). *The Savage Mind*. The Nature of Human Society Series. London: Weidenfeld & Nicolson.

Lévi-Strauss, Claude (1968). Introduction à l'oeuvre de Marcel Mauss. In

Marcel Mauss: Sociologie et anthropologie. Paris: Presses Universitaires de France, ix–lii.

Lévi-Strauss, Claude (1969a). *The Elementary Structures of Kinship*. London: Eyre & Spottiswoode.

Lévi-Strauss, Claude (1969b). *The Raw and the Cooked*. New York: Harper & Row.

Lienhardt, Godfrey (1982). The Dinka and catholicism. In J. Davis (ed.) *Religious Organization and Religious Experience*. London: Academic Press, 81–97.

Malinowski, Bronislaw (1922). *Argonauts of the Western Pacific. An Account of Native Enterprise and Adventures in the Archipelagoes of Melanesian New Guinea*. London: Routledge & Kegan Paul.

Malinowski, Bronislaw (1929). *The Sexual Life of Savages in North-Western Melanesia. An Ethnographic Account of Courtship, Marriage and Family Life among the Natives of the Trobriand Islands, British New Guinea*. London: Routledge & Kegan Paul.

Malinowski, Bronislaw (1965 [1935]). *Coral Gardens and their Magic, Vol. 1: Soil-Tilling and Agricultural Rites in the Trobriand Islands*. Bloomington: Indiana University Press.

Mauss, Marcel (1954). *The Gift. Forms and Functions of Exchange in Archaic Societies*, translated by Ian Cunnison. London: Cohen and West.

Mount, Ferdinand (1983). *The Subversive Family. An Alternative History of Love and Marriage*. London: Jonathan Cape.

Nightingale, Benedict (1973). *Charities*. London: Allen Lane.

Origo, Iris (1957). *A Measure of Love*. London: Jonathan Cape.

Pahl, Jan (1983). The allocation of money and the structuring of inequality within marriage. *Sociological Review*, 31, 239–62.

Pahl, Raymond Edward (1984). *Divisions of Labour*. Oxford: Blackwell.

Panoff, Michel (1970). Marcel Mauss's *The Gift* revisited. *Man* (n.s.), 5, 60.

Parry, Jonathan and Maurice Bloch (eds) (1989). *Money and the Morality of Exchange*. Cambridge: Cambridge University Press.

Pirenne, Henri (1925). *Medieval Cities*. Princeton: Princeton University Press.

Polanyi, Karl (1947). Our obsolete market mentality. *Commentary*, 3, 109–17.

Polanyi, Karl (1957). The economy as an instituted process. In Karl Polanyi, C. M. Arensberg and H. C. V. Pearson (eds) *Trade and Market in the Early Empires. Economies in History and Theory*. Glencoe, IL: Free Press.

Polanyi, Karl, C. M. Arensberg and H. C. V. Pearson (1957). *Trade and Market in the Early Empires. Economies in History and Theory*. Glencoe, IL: Free Press.

Pospisil, Leopold (1972). *Kapauku Papuan Economy*. Yale University Publications in Anthropology 67. New Haven, CT: Human Relations Area Files Press.

Robbins, Lionel (1932). *An Essay on the Nature and Significance of Economic Science*. London: Macmillan & Co.

Robbins, Lionel (1968). The subject matter of economics. In Edward E. LeClair and Harold K. Schneider (eds) *Economic Anthropology*. New York: Holt, Rinehart & Winston, 88–99.

Roberts, Bryan, Ruth Finnegan and Duncan Gallie (1985). *New Approaches to Economic Life. Economic Restructuring: Unemployment and the Social Division of Labour*. Manchester: Manchester University Press.

Rosman, Abraham and Paula Rubel (1971). *Feasting with Mine Enemy. Rank and Exchange among Northwest Coast Societies*. New York: Columbia University Press.

Sahlins, Marshall D. (1965). On the sociology of primitive exchange. In Michael Banton (ed.) *The Relevance of Models for Social Anthropology*. London: Tavistock Publications, 139–227. (Reprinted in Sahlins, *Stone Age Economics*. Chicago: Aldine-Atherton.)

Sahlins, Marshall D. (1972a). Exchange value and the diplomacy of primitive trade. In M. D. Sahlins, *Stone Age Economics*. Chicago: Aldine-Atherton, 277–314.

Sahlins, Marshall D. (1972b). *Stone Age Economics*. Chicago: Aldine-Atherton.

Salisbury, R. F. (1962). *From Stone to Steel. Economic Consequences of a Technological Change in New Guinea*. Melbourne: Melbourne University Press.

Samuelson, Paul A. (1966). Comment on Ernest Nagel's 'Assumptions in economic theory'. In J. E. Stiglitz (ed.) *The Collected Scientific Papers of Paul A. Samuelson*. Cambridge, Mass.: MIT Press.

Sawyer, Geoffrey (1965). *Law in Society*. Oxford: Clarendon Press.

Schieffelin, Edward L. (1980). Reciprocity and the construction of reality. *Man* (n.s.), 15, 502.

Schwimmer, Erik (1979). Reciprocity and structure: a semiotic analysis of some Orokaiva exchange data. *Man* (n.s.), 14, 271.

Sen, Amartya (1982). Rational fools: a critique of the behavioural foundations of economic theory. In Amartya Sen, *Choice, Welfare and Measurement*. Oxford: Blackwell, 84–108.

Silverman, Sydel F. (1977). Patronage as myth. In E. A. Gellner and J. Waterbury (eds) *Patrons and Clients*. London: Duckworth and Centre for Mediterranean Studies of AUFS.

Sperber, Dan (1975). *Rethinking Symbolism*. Cambridge: Cambridge University Press.

Strathern, Andrew (1971). *The Rope of Moka. Big-men and Ceremonial*

Exchange in Mount Hagen, New Guinea. Cambridge Studies in Social Anthropology 4. Cambridge: Cambridge University Press.

Strathern, Marilyn (1988). *The Gender of the Gift. Problems with Women and Problems with Society in Melanesia.* Berkeley: University of California Press.

Strecker, Ivo (1988). *The Social Practice of Symbolisation: An Anthropological Analysis.* London: Athlone Press.

Tilly, Charles (1985). War making and state making as organised crime. In D. Rueschmeyer, T. Skocpol and P. B. Evans (eds) *Bringing the State Back In.* Cambridge: Cambridge University Press.

Titmuss, Richard M. (1969). *The Gift Relationship. From Human Blood to Social Policy.* London: Routledge.

von Mises, Ludwig (1949). *Human Action. A Treatise of Economics.* New Haven, CT: Yale University Press.

Weiner, Annette B. (1976). *Women of Value, Men of Renown. New Perspectives in Trobriand Exchange.* Austin: University of Texas Press.

Wierzbicka, Anna (1984). Apples are not a 'kind of fruit': the semantics of human categorization. *American Ethnologist*, 11, 313–28.

Wilson, B. R. (ed.) (1970). *Rationality.* Oxford: Blackwell.

Wilson, D. A. (1927). *Carlyle at his Zenith, 1848–1853.* London: Kegan Paul.

Wilson, D. A. (1929). *Carlyle to Threescore-and-ten.* London: Kegan Paul.

Index